IS AMERICA FALLING APART?

America's Blessings are in Danger of Being Lost

AMERICA'S
CONTROVERSY
with
God's
COVENANT

★ ★ ★

PERRY STONE ★ BILL CLOUD

AMERICA'S
CONTROVERSY
with
God's
COVENANT

ISBN 978-0-9785920-5-9

First Edition Printing: January, 2015

Unless otherwise indicated, all Scripture quotations are from the New
King James Version®. © 1990, 1995 by Thomas Nelson Publishers,
Nashville, Tennessee. Used by permission. All rights reserved.

Italics in quotations, including Scripture, reflect the authors' added
emphasis.

Cover design and book layout by Michael Dutton

Printed in the United States of America

CONTENTS

Discerning the Times

*He answered and said to them, "When it is evening
you say, 'It will be fair weather, for the sky is red';
and in the morning, 'It will be foul weather today,
for the sky is red and threatening.' Hypocrites!
You know how to discern the face of the sky, but
you cannot discern the signs of the times."*

– Matthew 16:2-3

THAT WE ARE living in very perilous times, there can be no doubt. All around us we see political upheaval, the threat of economic collapse, war and the general deterioration of society under the weight of a politically-correct mindset and acute immorality. World-changing events that used to occur every few years or even every decade or so have become commonplace—in fact, almost a daily occurrence—making it obvious that mankind's decline and journey away from the Creator is on a fast track. Perhaps the world has finally reached the tipping point that sends us speedily toward global calamity.

For decades now, learned men have warned of this time, comparing what the Bible declares about the last days with current events so that we can properly discern how close we are to the end of the age. In the past there have been many times when it seemed that the end of all

1

things was at hand and that the final judgment was upon us only to see a reprieve—or so it would seem.

But once again we find ourselves, presumably, at that precipice poised to go over the edge at any moment; waiting for *that* event which would forever change the world as we know it. While we do not intend to make any dogmatic predictions here—perhaps we may yet have another reprieve—we nevertheless intend to demonstrate that the world has never been closer to the culmination of the age, the rise of the Beast, and the return of the Messiah than we are right now. The signs of the times are everywhere.

For instance, as we look to the Middle East we see that it has never been more volatile. At the same time, the West—particularly the United States—has never been more vulnerable. There is an important connection between the two situations, and should the current trends continue, the potential consequence does not bode well for the world. Yet looking at the situation from a strictly Biblical point of view, it makes sense and lines up perfectly with what we observe in the Scripture.

Specifically, the Bible declares that at the end of days an evil prince and Godless system will arise in the East and subjugate the entire world. Logic dictates, as does Biblical precedent, that this scenario can not materialize if the West is strong and resolute, meaning that for this Eastern power to arise the Western powers must decrease. Given the present circumstances, it would seem that all the proper conditions may exist for this unfortunate scenario to unfold just as the Bible has predicted.

If this is so, the question must be asked, "What has brought about the demise of the West and the rapid decline of the United States?" This is extremely important to know, because the demise of the U.S. would help explain how these radical Islamic groups have been able to gain so much power in such a short amount of time! Are we indeed witnessing the fall of America and the rise of the Beast? The answer to the question, at least to us, seems to be clear and can be expressed in something that President Ronald Reagan warned of some thirty years ago when he said:

"If we forget we are one nation under God, we will be a nation gone under."

Sadly, it would seem that we in the United States have neglected to heed that warning, and consequently, should probably brace ourselves for the inevitable disintegration of what once was the greatest nation on the planet. We pray that this does not happen; we pray that our countrymen will turn back to God and that He would grant us a pardon as He did with Nineveh. Yet we cannot ignore that instead of repenting in sackcloth and ash, our leaders and the nation's people may, like Pharaoh, harden their hearts against God.

If, God forbid, the latter occurred and the nation was destined for decline, who among the nations of the world would step into the power vacuum left behind? Would it be a people more noble and God-fearing? If so, where are they now? Or might it be a blood-thirsty despot eager to make war on God's people? More to the point: might a murderous regime flying a black banner rise and replace the nation whose banner is red, white and blue? Frankly, it is our opinion that if America does falter, there will be a tidal wave of oppression and tyranny throughout the world such as never before seen.

That possibility certainly exists, and if it happens, most likely it will be due to a lack of strong, moral leadership on the part of the United States; maybe even due to a lack of the United States altogether, at least one as we have known it. That, ladies and gentlemen, is what we intend to address here: to explore what is happening in America and try to understand the source of the affliction that plagues us. We want to look at what God seems to be saying to His people so that we can better understand what present circumstances mean for the Body of Messiah and for the world at large.

To do so will require that we go beyond the symptoms of the problem and probe for the cause, meaning that we will first address critical biblical principles that have a direct bearing on our topic. Because we believe that America was conceived by devout men who entered into covenant with God, we need to understand what it means to be in covenant with Him and what the ramifications might be if we break that covenant. As you will see, history and most certainly the Bible provide the answer.

While we may be confident of the unfortunate outcome for a nation that abandons God, the timing of these events cannot be known for certain. Still, it is our nature to search for and attempt to ascertain the "when" of these things. While we certainly don't pretend to know such details beyond any doubt and won't make any predictions, still, based on what Christ told the people in Matthew 16, we are encouraged to observe the tell-tale signs and to draw a logical conclusion concerning the times.

Consider that some of the best clues to the season we live in may be found just above our heads. In other words, to understand the timing of these things, it could be as simple as looking at and discerning the face of the sky. More to the point; consider that at the end of each day, as the sun begins to set, its retreat announces the rising moon and the approaching night. So then, in terms of prophecy and what awaits the world, the light diminishing in the West signals the onset of darkness. Based on what we can currently observe in the world, and particularly the U.S., it would seem that this is happening now.

If the light of liberty and the glory of America are fading, her demise will serve to hasten the advancing darkness and the rising moon – the crescent moon no less. We see this happening presently in the East as millions of Islamists rally under a dark, black banner. It would seem that soon it will be dark, and along with that darkness the world will suffer the grip of tyranny, violence and, eventually, tribulation. Very soon, dear reader, it may be too dark for any of us to work at all (Jn. 9:4). Therefore, our effort here is to rightly divide the Word of Truth, discern the signs of the times, and come to the proper conclusion so that we may commit ourselves to the proper action. In a word, that is *repent*. So let us begin now.

CHAPTER 1

The Covenant and the Commandments

"Now therefore, if you will indeed obey my voice and keep my covenant, then you shall be a special treasure to me above all people; for all the earth is mine. And you shall be to me a kingdom of priests and a holy nation. These are the words which you shall speak to the children of Israel."

– EXODUS 19:5-6

IN THE SCRIPTURE above God tells Israel that they shall be His "special treasure"—His jewels—among all nations *if* they keep His covenant, indicating that this privileged status is predicated upon the responsibility to be true to God and to His ways. This means that Israel's election and designation as "chosen" was never conditioned on their ethnicity alone but on their commitment to be true to God's call and to live according to the faith handed down to them from Abraham.

In Genesis 15, Abraham was told to take certain animals and fowl, cut them into pieces and arrange them, presumably, upon an altar. After chasing away the birds of prey that wished to feast on this offering, the Bible says:

> "And it came to pass, when the sun went down and it was dark, that behold, there appeared a smoking oven and a burning torch that passed between those pieces. On the same day the LORD made a covenant with Abram, saying: 'To your descendants I have given this land, from the river of Egypt to the great river, the River Euphrates.'"
>
> – GENESIS 15:17-18

The Hebrew word translated here as *covenant* (*b'rit*) is used almost 300 times in the biblical text. It means "to bind in an agreement, to cut, to divide." Dividing or cutting, of course, refers to the cutting of animals and the shedding of blood as we see in the passage above.

The first such occurrence in the Bible is in the very beginning when God cut Man's side, removed a rib, and used that rib to create Woman. After he had created Woman, the Bible tells us that:

> "He brought her to the man. And Adam said, 'This is now bone of my bones and flesh of my flesh; she shall be called Woman because she was taken out of Man.'"
>
> – GENESIS 2:22-23

Following this passage the Bible tells us that Man has responsibility to the Woman; he is to leave his father and mother and cleave unto her. Thus we see that the first cutting and shedding of blood denotes the very first covenant in the history of the world. Moreover, the covenant between a husband and his wife is also seen as the two entering into that covenant before God that they may fulfill His purpose for their union—to be fruitful and multiply—or if we may put it this way, to produce life. This is an important point that we will revisit later.

PURPOSE OF COVENANT

Where the nation of Israel is concerned, it was the cutting of the Passover Lamb; its blood posted upon their doors was the sign—the mark of the covenant—that delivered them from the hand of Pharaoh. Subsequent to their escape from Egypt, God brought them to Mount Sinai and presented to them His contract—the Law, or better the

Torah. According to the terms, if they lived by His Word and instructions it would demonstrate to the world, and more importantly to Him, that they were His people.

Consequently, along with this special designation and responsibility to live according to the contract, came the purpose — to faithfully represent God to the rest of the nations that they might turn to Him as well. It is synonymous with the call given to Abraham when God said:

> "I will make you a great nation; I will bless you and make your name great; and you shall be a blessing. I will bless those who bless you, and I will curse him who curses you; and in you all the families of the earth shall be blessed."
>
> — GENESIS 12:2-3

In other words, because Abraham answered the call and accepted the challenge, God made a covenant with him, promising to bless him. However, as we see, this call and blessing was that he might also be a source of blessing for others — all the families of the earth. This same concept can be found in the New Testament when Peter writes to the Body:

> "You are a chosen generation, a royal priesthood, a holy nation. His own special people, that you may proclaim the praises of Him who called you out of darkness into His marvelous light."
>
> — 1 PETER 2:9

First of all notice that Peter echoes the same message God presented to Israel in Exodus and consequently the same challenge. We are not chosen because of what we are; we have been chosen to become what we are supposed to be — conformed to the image of the Son — and to inspire others to do the same.

When we emerge from the darkness of sin and live by His Word, we produce fruit. That fruit is intended to be a witness to those still in darkness that they too may come into His light; that they may inherit eternal life. In this way we become a source of blessing for the families of the earth. Messiah put it this way:

"Go therefore and make disciples of all the nations, baptizing them in the name of the Father and of the Son and of the Holy Spirit, teaching them to observe all things that I have commanded you."

– Matthew 28:19-20

Responsibility of the Covenant

The point is then that a covenant is more than just an agreement or contract—people break contracts everyday. A covenant is a matter of honor and responsibility, first to God and then to others. As an example, consider that marriage is a covenantal relationship and responsibility that should not be entered into lightly. It is not something that should be taken on and tossed off depending on our mood and our whims at that moment.

On most days, marriage is a tremendous challenge that serves to transform the husband and wife into something better than what they were in the beginning of the relationship. In a successful marriage, both husband and wife learn to sacrifice their own needs for the sake of the other, pledging their very life to them.

If they rise to the challenge and remain faithful to each other and the covenant, not only will they be blessed, but others will find a resource for wisdom and a fount of blessing. If the relationship between husband and wife is that important, how much more so is a covenantal relationship between a man and God, or a nation and God?

Therefore, when God made a covenant with Israel, it was not to acknowledge them as a special people as much as it was to challenge them to *become* a special people and to fulfill a special purpose. First and foremost, Israel's responsibility—and our responsibility—is to the God of Abraham, Isaac and Jacob; to live in the manner He has determined, that we bring honor to Him in the sight of all the nations. To do so is integral according to the terms of the covenant.

Secondly, but nevertheless equivalent to the first requirement, is the duty to our fellow man—the nations. You see, if God's people fail in the latter, that is to be a faithful witness to the nations and to make disciples, then they have failed in the former and will not fulfill the mandate given to them by God. In short, they will have broken the covenant.

Heart of the Covenant

In reality, the essence of the covenant boils down to the principle contained in these verses:

> "If someone says 'I love God,' and hates his brother, he is a liar; for he who does not love his brother whom he has seen, how can he love God whom he has not seen?"
>
> — 1 John 4:20

Jesus said:

> "'You shall love the Lord your God with all your heart, with all your soul, and with all your mind.' This is the first and great commandment. And the second is like it: 'You shall love your neighbor as yourself.' On these two commandments hang all the law and the prophets."
>
> — Matthew 22:37–40

Because Messiah likens the second commandment unto the first, the implication is that if you do not love your neighbor as yourself—if you are not committed to bringing him out of darkness into light—then how can you say you love God with all your heart? You can't. Therefore, if you don't love God in the proper way, then who and what do you love? The answer is most likely, "self." When that is the case, instead of bringing honor to God's Name, He is dishonored; instead of being a light to the nations, one becomes the object of accusation and ridicule.

> "When they came to the nations, wherever they went, they profaned My holy name—when they said of them, 'These are the people of the LORD, and yet they have gone out of His land.'"
>
> — Ezekiel 36:20

Contrast this selfish approach to the covenant with the love that God has for mankind and His faithfulness to keep the covenant to us.

He so loved the world that He sent His own Son to die that those who believed on Him might have life. Jesus' commitment to the Father's will was such that on the eve of His crucifixion He was compelled to say:

> "This cup is the new covenant in My blood which is shed for you."
>
> – LUKE 22:20

And so we see that a covenant is born out of love. It is a commitment so strong that it can only be consummated if blood is shed —because "the life is in the blood"—indicating that a covenant is a commitment of one's very life to another. In this case, the One cutting the covenant is willing to shed His blood, that is to say, to lay down his life for the other—for you and me.

In response, the other party also agrees to lay down his or her life for the sake of the one offering the covenant. Where God's people are concerned, laying down our life means refraining from doing our will and living our way, while committing ourselves to live by God's instructions and His way of life—His commandments. By this, we show that we really do love Him. Remember, Jesus said:

> "If you love Me, keep my commandments."
>
> – JOHN 14:15

Because He "so loved the world" and brought us into this covenant, we should also be committed to love our neighbor as ourselves as He has commanded us. If we falter in this commandment and continue unrepentant, we will eventually break another commandment, specifically, the greatest of all commandments—to love God with all our heart. When this process has run its course, unfortunately, we will be found to have turned away from God completely and to have abandoned His covenant.

To underscore the danger of selfishness and lack of concern for our fellow man, it is noteworthy to recall that God's final assessment of Sodom was not what most people would assume. Obviously their sinful deeds brought about their destruction, but what brought about their sinful deeds?

> "Look, this was the iniquity of your sister Sodom: She and her daughter had pride, fullness of food, and abundance of idleness; neither did she strengthen the hand of the poor and needy."
>
> – EZEKIEL 16:49

In no way are we trying to suggest that Sodom's other infamous deeds were of no consequence; to the contrary, we are suggesting that their violent and perverse lifestyle may have been the fruit of a self-absorbed society concerned only for themselves with no regard for others. In other words, when people—whether individuals or nations—justify breaking one of God's commands, it will lead to breaking other commandments and eventually the covenant He has made with them.

When Man and Woman entered into covenant, they were given specific instructions—"Be fruitful and multiply, fill the earth and subdue it." (Gen. 1:28). Adam was given instruction related to the covenant that only he could fulfill—to "cleave unto his wife." At some point Adam must have faltered in this. How else would the Adversary have been able to seduce Eve in the way he did had Adam remained close by her side? Therefore, because he failed in this commandment, he broke yet another commandment and consequently broke the covenant with God.

ENGRAVED IN STONE, WRITTEN IN OUR HEARTS

This now brings us to another point. Though there is a distinction between God's commandments and the covenant with God, they nevertheless fit hand in glove.

The Hebrew word *commandment* (*mitzvah*) is mentioned 171 times in Scripture and is a "divine law and injunction from God to man." When a man obeys these laws he is blessed, as are others. For instance, Abraham obeyed God's commandments and all nations are blessed as a consequence (Gen. 26:5). Scripture also tells us that God extends mercy to those who love Him and keep His commandments (Ex. 20:6).

It could be said that the commandments of God were written in stone, while the covenant is a matter of the heart, born of love and consummated by blood for the cause of eternal life. While this is true, it is also written that one day God will write His commandments upon the hearts of those who are in covenant with Him.

> "This is the covenant that I will make with the house of Israel after those days, says the Lord: I will put my law in their minds and write it on their hearts and I will be their God, and they shall be my people."
>
> – JEREMIAH 31:33

The point would be this: one who is in covenant with God will keep His commandments. If God reigns in their heart, His commandments will reign in their life because they rein in their selfish inclinations. In short, His commandments will be written in our heart, because He is in our heart.

Therefore, we do not keep His commandments in order to be saved and enter into the covenant, rather we keep His commandments because we are already saved and already in covenant with Him. As a demonstration of our love and devotion to Him, and because we are committed to the covenant, we walk in obedience to His Word, thus demonstrating the inter-relationship between commandment and covenant.

As we said before, our keeping His covenant is why we are regarded as His special treasure, and the purpose of being that treasure is that we might be a source of light and blessing to the rest of the world. When we fail to be the proper example to the world, it is likely because we have failed to live the proper lifestyle unto God. This is true with individuals and with nations as well.

In that vein, history has proven that no person or nation makes the jump from being predominantly righteous to being predominately wicked overnight. It is typically a gradual process. Therefore, in order for the people of God or for a nation to come to the place where they are breaking His covenant, it must first mean they have already, and for some time, been taking the liberty of breaking His commandments.

WHEN THERE IS NO REPENTANCE

It is, unfortunately, man's nature to redefine laws—commandments if you will—in order to accommodate his preferred lifestyle. In other words, rather than adjusting his errant deeds to conform to the reality of God's laws, he will move or erase the boundaries of law so as to include that which he doesn't wish to change about his life.

If he can't or won't rein in his evil inclination, he will ignore that which would indict his passion; evil will become good, and good will become evil. Over time, he convinces himself that his view of reality *is* reality, hardening his heart to God's correction.

History testifies that each and every time God's people felt justified in breaking His commandments and ignoring His laws, before it was too late, He would send warnings to urge them to abandon their ill-fated path, calling them to return to Him and to His Word. Sadly, they almost always continued in their disregard for His admonition, and after decades of breaking His commandments, eventually broke His covenant.

Only then—when the bride had forsaken her husband for others—do we see that God allowed their strength to wane. Only then did He permit their enemies to invade and overrun them and force them from their land. Only then did they realize that God was no longer with them. That unfortunate result is what we now turn our attention to.

CHAPTER TWO

The Sign of the Covenant

*"And I will make my covenant between me and
you, and I will multiply you exceedingly."*

— GENESIS 17:2

A S WE HAVE already noted, most biblical covenants involve the cutting of flesh and are sealed in blood. The blood, of course, is symbolic of the "life" that exists within the blood. Yet, there is the other aspect of it as well — cutting or removing flesh. For instance, when God affirmed the covenant with Abraham, it was through the rite of circumcision.

> "This is My covenant which you shall keep, between Me and you and your descendants after you: every male child among you shall be circumcised; and you shall be circumcised in the flesh of your foreskins, and it shall be a sign of the covenant between Me and you. He who is eight days old among you shall be circumcised, every male child in your generations, he who is born in your house or bought with money from any foreigner who is not your descendant. He who is born in your house and he who is bought with your money must be circumcised, and My covenant shall be in your flesh for an everlasting covenant. And the uncircumcised male child, who is not circumcised in the flesh of his foreskin, that person shall be cut off from his people; he has broken My covenant."
>
> — GENESIS 17:10-14

First, please note that God made the covenant with Abraham AND his descendants after him—later known as Israel. To be regarded as part of this family, however, it was required that the males remove a piece of flesh from their bodies through circumcision. In part, this speaks to the essence of the covenant God has made with His people: He commits completely to them and desires that they reciprocate in like manner—"love the LORD with ALL your heart."

GOD STAKES HIS REPUTATION FOR THE SAKE OF COVENANT

For His part we see that the covenant is backed by the eternal authority of God's Name. In fact, sixteen times the name *Yahweh* is used in conjunction with the covenant He made with Israel; you could say it is His covenant name. One example of this is found when God introduced Himself to Moses.

> "And God spoke to Moses and said to him: 'I am the LORD. I appeared to Abraham, to Isaac, and to Jacob, as God Almighty, but by My name LORD I was not known to them. I have also established My covenant with them, to give them the land of Canaan, the land of their pilgrimage, in which they were strangers. And I have also heard the groaning of the children of Israel whom the Egyptians keep in bondage, and I have remembered My covenant. Therefore say to the children of Israel: I am the LORD; I will bring you out from under the burdens of the Egyptians...'"
>
> – EXODUS 6:2-6

The importance of these verses in our context is that God was linking His Sacred Name, *Yahweh*, to the covenant made with the patriarchs and now the nation of Israel. In other words, He was putting His reputation as the Eternal One and only true Sovereign on the line in the sight of the entire universe. If He didn't keep His part of the covenant, His Name would be profaned, and He wasn't about to let that happen. Consequently, the covenant with His people is backed by His Word, which, according to Isaiah, does not fail.

"So shall My word be that goes forth from My mouth; it shall not return to Me void, but it shall accomplish what I please, and it shall prosper in the thing for which I sent it."

– Isaiah 55:11

The Psalmist said:

"My covenant I will not break, nor alter the word that has gone out of My lips."

– Psalms 89:34

The fact that this has always been and remains true today, explains why the empires and nations that have come against Israel, Jerusalem and His people suffer calamity and eventually die.

When Pharaoh pursued Israel into the sea, it cost Egypt 600 chariots, 50,000 horsemen, and 200,000 footmen; not to mention that Egypt has NEVER regained the power and grandeur she enjoyed before touching God's anointed. When the Assyrians laid siege to Jerusalem, the result was that 185,000 of them were slain by a plague sent by an angel. The Babylonians, though once one of the greatest empires known to man, were defeated and vanquished in one night because of their contempt for God and His people.

The list continues on: the Greeks were defeated by the Maccabees and eventually declined; the Romans, though great in power and influence, were eventually overrun by Barbarians and devolved into economic decay. Nation after nation has come and gone, shining brightly for a moment but then fading into oblivion never to recover their past glory. The prophet noted:

"They are dead, they will not live; they are deceased, they will not rise. Therefore you have punished and destroyed them, and made all their memory to perish. You have increased the nation, O LORD, you have increased the nation; you are glorified; you have expanded all the borders of the land."

– Isaiah 26:14-15

Yet, consider Israel. At one time she was considered to be a conquered and extinct nation, but as we know, Israel still exists! In Hebrew it would be said, "Am Yisrael chai!" — "The people of Israel live!" Here is why: Israel, Jerusalem and God's people have a Divine covenant with the Creator of the Universe. Attack them and it is equivalent to attacking God Himself. And as we pointed out earlier, God keeps His covenant because it is His Name, His Word and His reputation that are on the line.

THE FLESH CANNOT PLEASE GOD

Thus we conclude that, without fail, God has been true to keep His covenant with His people. So, what does He want from us? — that we would "love the LORD with ALL your heart," and be faithful to the covenant. Let's put it this way: the reason we were born again was so that in and through the Messiah, we could learn how to die — to our flesh.

As we know, flesh is emblematic of a carnal nature — our desires, passions and inclinations. We also know one cannot please God if he gives in to the deeds of the flesh. Paul said:

> "The carnal mind is enmity against God; for it is not subject to the law of God, nor indeed can be. So then, those who are in the flesh cannot please God."
>
> – ROMANS 8:7-8

This concept brings us back to the rite of circumcision and the covenant made with Abraham and his seed — the removal of flesh and how it hints at cost incurred on us if we are to be in covenant with God. If we are to be faithful, we must die to ourselves and our carnal desires everyday. Jesus said:

> "If anyone desires to come after Me, let him deny himself, and take up his cross daily and follow Me. For whoever desires to save his life will lose it, but whoever loses his life for My sake will save it."
>
> – LUKE 9:23-24

Our flesh has to be crucified, and we must be willing to present ourselves as a "living sacrifice," saying "no" to our will. Moreover, this requires more than just a cut in the flesh of our physical body; actually it is something that should be conceived and manifested in our heart. Moses said to Israel:

> "Therefore circumcise the foreskin of your heart, and be stiff-necked no longer."
>
> — DEUTERONOMY 10:16

Later He said:

> "And the LORD your God will circumcise your heart and the heart of your descendants, to love the LORD your God with all your heart and with all your soul that you may live."
>
> — DEUTERONOMY 30:6

It is clear that circumcision of the heart was what God desired and intended from the very beginning. Yes, He required that Abraham and his seed fulfill the physical aspect of this as well but, as we are admonished to acknowledge, the physical manifestation is given to teach us of the spiritual principle (1 Cor. 15:46). It also becomes clear that it is impossible for us to love God with **all** our hearts until and unless our hearts have been circumcised by God. That would also indicate that, unless we have been circumcised in our hearts, we cannot be faithful to the covenant with God.

We can say we love God, can call ourselves believers, and can display the trappings that go along with being a God-fearer. However, as Paul points out, that means nothing if the outward signs are not a true reflection of the heart.

> "For he is not a Jew who is one outwardly, nor is circumcision that which is outward in the flesh; but he is a Jew who is one inwardly; and circumcision is that of the heart, in the Spirit, not in the letter; whose praise is not from men but from God."
>
> — ROMANS 2:28-29

19

A Sign between God and His People

This discussion has been intended to bring us to this all-important point: true circumcision is designated by God to be a sign (Hebrew *ote*) of the covenant between Him and Abraham and those identifying themselves as the seed of Abraham. In Genesis 17, the Hebrew root word for *sign* means, "to communicate; signaling." The Bible uses this term to indicate a "mark, token or monument." Thus, it is the marker that says to the Creator and to the world, "I belong to the God of Abraham, Isaac and Jacob," something that is not to be taken lightly.

The word *ote* is, in fact, used to signify an "emblem, ensign or flag." Perhaps we could put it this way: in God's eyes circumcision of the heart represents the flag or emblem to which you pledge your loyalty and allegiance. It signifies that you have chosen to identify with the God of Israel, with His people and the nation He has ordained.

Furthermore, it declares that you are committed to following His laws given to that nation for the betterment of yourself and your fellow man; you believe in this relationship so strongly that you are willing to commit your life to it, because you love Him with all your heart, soul and strength. So then, what does this say of those in Abraham's family who refused to be circumcised in their flesh or, more importantly, in their heart?

> "The uncircumcised male child, who is not circumcised in the flesh of his foreskin, that person shall be cut off from his people; he has broken My covenant."
>
> – Genesis 17:14

The person who refuses to be circumcised is the person who refuses to remove, or deny, the flesh, and as we read in Romans 8, that person cannot please God. In fact, according to Paul, that person is hostile toward God. He doesn't wish to be considered part of God's family (nation).

Think of it this way: how does it make you feel to see someone desecrate, maybe even burn, the American flag? How does it make you feel to hear Americans, living in America, ridiculing and mocking the emblem that represents so many others who have come before them and who gave their lives for what that emblem represents?

Now imagine how God feels when His people break the covenant He has been so committed to. When God's people forsake His covenant, it exceeds the disgraceful actions of those Americans who take the stars and stripes, throw it on the ground, trample it and then burn it. They are saying, "We want no part of what this represents." Likewise, when we disregard and break God's covenant, we are saying "We want no part of this," and where God's covenant is concerned, that can be very dangerous.

A MATTER OF LIFE AND DEATH

The use of the word *ote* as a sign is also used in another critical period in Israel's history—during the first Passover in Egypt. In anticipation of leaving the bondage of Egypt, God instructed them to take a male lamb of the first year, slaughter it on a particular day, and then take its blood and post it upon their doors as a sign.

> "For I will pass through the land of Egypt on that night, and will strike all the firstborn in the land of Egypt, both man and beast; and against all the gods of Egypt I will execute judgment: I am the LORD. Now the blood shall be a sign (Hebrew *ote*) for you on the houses where you are. And when I see the blood, I will pass over you; and the plague shall not be on you to destroy you when I strike the land of Egypt."
>
> – EXODUS 12:12-13

Later, Moses would reaffirm this promise and indicate that the blood would protect them from the Destroyer.

> "For the LORD will pass through to strike the Egyptians; and when He sees the blood on the lintel and on the two doorposts, the LORD will pass over the door and not allow the destroyer to come into your houses to strike you."
>
> – EXODUS 12:23

What we glean from this particular example is that the sign between God and us—in this case, the blood of the Passover Lamb—means the difference between life and death. To ignore the requirements whereby the sign would be present is to invite death and destruction into your home and family—and your nation. So, to some degree, the choice to live or to die is left to us.

> "Behold, I set before you today a blessing and a curse: the blessing, if you obey the commandments of the LORD your God which I command you today; and the curse, if you do not obey the commandments of the LORD your God, but turn aside from the way which I command you today, to go after other gods which you have not known."
>
> – DEUTERONOMY 11:26-28

> "I call heaven and earth as witnesses today against you, that I have set before you life and death, blessing and cursing; therefore choose life, that both you and your descendants may live."
>
> – DEUTERONOMY 30:19

A nation who keeps His commandments is a nation in covenant with Him—a blessed nation.

> "Blessed is the nation whose God is the LORD, The people He has chosen as His own inheritance."
>
> – PSALM 33:12

But those who turn to other gods and refuse to keep His commandments, disgrace the sign between them and God. Those who abandon the covenant have either ignorantly or defiantly invited curses, death and destruction into their borders.

Understanding the life and death significance of the blood upon the door, coupled with the sign of circumcision and its relevance to the covenant, we can safely deduce that to break covenant with God leads to eventual death. To abandon God and His ways is equivalent to approaching the Tree of the Knowledge of Good and Evil and willfully eating of its deadly fruit. The result can only be one thing—exile from God and from the blessing He had previously bestowed upon those once in fellowship with Him. With that in mind, let us examine more closely what happens to a nation that does just that—rejects His

Word, ignores the sign between it and God, breaks His covenant, and turns to other gods, other philosophies, and carnal pursuits.

CHAPTER THREE

Breaking Covenant

*"If you despise My statutes, or if your soul
abhors My judgments, so that you do not
perform all My commandments, but break
My covenant, I also will do this to you."*

– LEVITICUS 26:15-16

THUS FAR WE have discussed the importance of the covenant and why His people should never forsake it. But what actually happens when they do? What are the indicators that let us know a person or a nation has abandoned God and His covenant? Before we look at that, for comparison's sake, let's first look at the blessings promised to the nation that keeps His commandments and His covenant.

> "If you walk in My statutes and keep My commandments, and perform them, then I will give you rain in its season, the land shall yield its produce, and the trees of the field shall yield their fruit. Your threshing shall last till the time of vintage, and the vintage shall last till the time of sowing; you shall eat your bread to the full, and dwell in your land safely. I will give peace in the land, and you shall lie down, and none will make you afraid; I will rid the land of evil beasts, and the sword will not go through your land. You will chase your enemies, and they shall fall by the sword before you. Five of you shall chase a hundred, and a hundred of you shall put ten thousand to flight; your enemies shall

fall by the sword before you. For I will look on you favorably and make you fruitful, multiply you and confirm My covenant with you."

– LEVITICUS 26:3-9

In short, a nation in covenant with God is assured peace, prosperity and power. In sharp contrast, look at what befalls the nation that abandons the covenant.

"I will even appoint terror over you, wasting disease and fever which shall consume the eyes and cause sorrow of heart. And you shall sow your seed in vain, for your enemies shall eat it. I will set My face against you, and you shall be defeated by your enemies. Those who hate you shall reign over you, and you shall flee when no one pursues you. And after all this, if you do not obey Me, then I will punish you seven times more for your sins. I will break the pride of your power; I will make your heavens like iron and your earth like bronze. And your strength shall be spent in vain; for your land shall not yield its produce, nor shall the trees of the land yield their fruit."

– LEVITICUS 26:16-20

In short, the peace, prosperity and power once enjoyed will be taken from them and be replaced with fear, lack and weakness. That is just the beginning. The text goes on to say that, if still unrepentant, the nation will suffer attacks by wild beasts, loss of livestock, deserted highways and, eventually, "the sword" that "will execute the vengeance of the covenant" and "pestilence" (Leviticus 26:25). Any of these curses would be bad enough, but these last two, in light of recent events, are terrifyingly familiar when considering today's world.

Before examining the present, though, let us look back and see specifically what God told Israel would happen when they abandoned the covenant, why it happened, and how it actually unfolded.

THE BEGINNING DESCRIBES THE END

As we begin this segment of our study, it is important to recall a fundamental principle contained in the Scripture: if you want to understand what is happening today or to understand what is going to happen tomorrow, you must go back and review what has already happened. For instance, in Isaiah it says:

> "Remember this, and show yourselves men; Recall to mind O you transgressors. Remember the former things of old, for I am God, and there is no other. I am God and there is none like me, declaring the end from the beginning, and from ancient times things that are not yet done, saying my counsel shall stand."
>
> – ISAIAH 46:8–10

Another example of this concept is found in Ecclesiastes.

> "That which is has already been, and what is to be has already been; and God requires an account of what is past."
>
> – ECCLESIASTES 3:15

These verses, along with others, make it very clear that in telling us the beginning of all things, God actually describes to us the end of all things. Isaiah and Solomon are not suggesting that God predicted the end way back in the beginning but that He describes the end by telling us the beginning. Therefore, if we want to properly interpret the signs around us and discern what they are telling us about our present state and our potential future, then we must go back into the past and see how God dealt with Israel in similar circumstances.

One such example is found in the book of Deuteronomy as Moses addresses the children of Israel just before they entered into the land of Canaan. As we examine the text, it is important to remember that Moses' words are not exclusive to the Israelites of long ago. They are just as relevant to our present day and circumstance, because according to Scripture, the end is the beginning and the beginning is the end. In fact, the Apostle Paul indicated that everything written in the beginning was "for our learning" (Rom. 15:4).

MAN'S EVIL INCLINATION

> "And the Lord said to Moses: 'Behold, you will rest with your fathers; and this people will rise and play the harlot with the gods of the foreigners of the land, where they go to be among them

and they will forsake me and break my covenant which I have made with them.'"

— Deuteronomy 31:16

The very first thing we want to note here is the statement that is made concerning Israel—"they will forsake me and break my covenant." As we've already noted, there are dire consequences for those who break covenant with God. Furthermore, as we have also noted, to get to that point betrays the fact that these are people who have become self-absorbed and have consistently given in to their own carnal desires and passions.

The second thing we want to note here is that God made this declaration before Israel crossed over the Jordan River. Before they even took possession of the land, God already knew what was really in their hearts and that they would eventually turn from Him. In fact, later in this same chapter, He says:

> "I know the inclination of their behavior today, even before I have brought them to the land of which I swore to give them."

— Deuteronomy 31:21

There is another passage in Deuteronomy in which we see this same truth, that is, that God perceives the intent of man's heart even before they follow through with their deeds. When God spoke to Israel at Mount Sinai, the elders of Israel went to Moses requesting that God cease speaking to them out of fear that if He continued they would die. They pledged that if Moses would speak to God on their behalf, when he returned with God's words, they would "hear and do." Moses would later recall:

> "Then the Lord heard the voice of your words you spoke to me, and the Lord said to me, 'I have heard the voice of the words of this people which they've spoken to you. They are right in all that they have spoken. Oh, that they had such a heart in them that they would fear me and always keep my commandments, that it might be well with them and with their children forever!'"

— Deuteronomy 5:28-29

Once again, we see that even before men act upon that which they harbor within their heart, God already knows what they intend to do. He already knows whether or not they are committed to the covenant because, as He declared in the beginning:

"The imagination of man's heart is evil from his youth."

– Genesis 8:21

Perhaps we could phrase it this way—only God can recognize a heart that is circumcised and distinguish it from the one that is not. He knows that the uncircumcised heart will eventually be hardened toward Him and His will. He knows that those whose hearts are not pliable and sensitive to His voice will eventually turn completely away from Him and break His covenant. So it would be with Israel.

"Then my anger shall be aroused against them in that day, and I will forsake them, and I will hide my face from them, and they shall be devoured."

– Deuteronomy 31:17

This portion of the verse shows us the consequence that befalls the people or nation that turn away from God, forsake Him and break His covenant. He forsakes them and turns his face from them. Of course, this harsh response is just that—a response. He reacts to their action; He turns from them because they have first turned away from Him, following after the inclination of their own heart.

If He determined to hide His face from them—this would be synonymous with turning His back to them—it is because they first turned their face, attention and desire to other gods, other ideas and philosophies. This, of course, is nothing new; in fact, it happened in the beginning.

BLESSINGS AND CURSES, LIFE AND DEATH

The Bible tells us that, in the midst of the Garden of Eden, there existed two prominent trees—the Tree of Life and the Tree of the Knowledge of Good and Evil. The former tree rendered a fruit that, if you were to eat it, you would live forever. We know this is true because

29

after man had fallen, God set cherubim to guard the way to the Tree of Life lest the man take hold of it, eat of its fruit and live forever (Gen. 3:22).

The latter tree, which was a mingled tree, produced a fruit that rendered death. In fact, God said:

> "But of the tree of the knowledge of good and evil you shall not eat, for in the day that you eat of it you shall surely die."
>
> – GENESIS 2:17

Again, both of these trees grew in the midst of the Garden of Eden, so it is conceivable that these trees grew in close proximity to each other. If that be the case, then it could be said that Adam was faced with the choice between blessings and curses, life and death.

If Adam had continued to partake of the Tree of Life, ignoring the Tree of the Knowledge of Good and Evil, he would have presumably lived forever. This is a very important point to consider, because the Tree of Life is emblematic of the Word of God. In Proverbs it says of wisdom:

> "She is a tree of life to those who take hold of her, and happy are all who retain her."
>
> – PROVERBS 3:18

It is understood in Judaism that wisdom (Hebrew word *khochmah*) is synonymous with the Word of God. As a matter of fact, in most every synagogue you will find what is called in Hebrew an *aron*, or Ark. This particular ark houses a Torah scroll upon which is written the books of Moses, which is the Word of God.

At certain times during the congregational service, the ark is opened, the Torah scroll is removed and the Word of God is read before the people. When the Torah scroll is returned to its resting place within the Ark, the congregation stands and chants an ancient liturgical prayer.

Etz chayim hi, lama chazikimba, v'tomcheha m'ushar...

"It is a tree of life to those who take hold of it, and those who support it are praiseworthy."

The point of bringing this out is to underscore the fact that the Tree of Life in the midst of the Garden of Eden represents the Word of God—the source of life. As long as we partake of its fruit, that is, as long as we are faithful to keep His instructions and commandments, we will live. Furthermore, as believers in Messiah, we understand that the Word of God became flesh and dwelt among us (John 1:14). Therefore, the Tree of Life is also emblematic of the Messiah, Jesus, who said:

"I have come that they may have life, and that they may have it more abundantly."

– JOHN 10:10

The Tree of Life represents Christ, and as long as we receive Him, focus upon Him, follow Him and allow Him to live in and through us, we will inherit eternal life. As we crucify our flesh, learning to deny ourselves that He may be manifest in us, we more closely resemble His image instead of that which is mortal and corruptible flesh. To those who commit to this lofty goal He says:

"To him who overcomes I will give to eat from the tree of life, which is in the midst of the Paradise of God."

– REVELATION 2:7

"Blessed are those who do His commandments that they may have the right to the tree of life, and may enter through the gates into the city."

– REVELATION 22:14

On the other hand, if we begin to turn away from Him and from His Word, we, by default, gaze upon the other tree—the one that produces death. This is the inclination that we inherited from our father, Adam, and why we had to be born again. When Eve looked upon the Tree of the Knowledge of Good and Evil, being seduced by the Serpent, she ultimately concluded that this tree was pleasant to the sight, good for food and a tree desirable to make one wise (Gen. 3:6). At that point, she took of its fruit and ate it. Then, turning to her husband, she gave Adam the fruit, which he ate.

The point is this: for man to determine that the forbidden fruit was pleasant to look upon must mean that he was looking upon it. For man to determine that the fruit of the forbidden tree was good for food must mean that he desired it. Finally, for man to determine that this forbidden tree was desirable to attain wisdom (Hebrew *khochmah*) must mean that he studied it intently. In other words, for man to focus upon the forbidden tree must mean that he first turned his face away from the Tree of Life.

And so we see that when God foretold of Israel's future backsliding and turning away from Him to embrace other things — things that render death — it was nothing new for God's people. They had been doing it from the beginning. They would indeed go into the land and possess it. They would enjoy the blessings of the land and grow fat off of what it had to offer, but they would eventually turn their face from Him and toward other gods, thus breaking His covenant.

> "When I have brought them to the land flowing with milk and honey, of which I swore to their fathers, and they have eaten and filled themselves and grown fat, then they will turn to other gods and serve them; and they will provoke me and break my covenant."
>
> – DEUTERONOMY 31:20

We should point out here that each and every time God's people begin to look around and desire what is forbidden, it almost always looks good, at least initially. It might even seem to be the right thing to do, perhaps even appearing to offer a way to know everything God knows concerning good and evil. However, by the time the hidden evil is revealed, it is typically too late. The deed is done; the covenant is broken.

WHEN GOD REMOVES HIS PRESENCE

Twice in Deuteronomy 31 — once in verse 17 and again in verse 18 — God tells Israel that because they have turned from Him, He would turn His face from them. Moreover, He says:

> "I will surely hide my face in that day because of all the evil which they have done, in that they have turned to other gods."
>
> – DEUTERONOMY 31:18

Imagine, if you will, a child who is behaving in an unruly manner, ignoring every plea from his mother to correct his behavior. To the contrary, the child acts even worse, growing increasingly belligerent toward his mother's stern warnings. He interrupts adult conversation; he talks back to his elders, and in general, disregards every instruction he's ever been taught by his parents.

Now imagine that the mother, furious with his behavior, turns her back on her child, ignoring his rude attempts at getting her attention. This response to his misbehavior is to signal to him that until he corrects his ways and behaves in the manner he has been taught, he no longer has access to her; she has turned her face away from him.

This illustration is to suggest that, in a manner of speaking, this is exactly what God was trying to convey to Israel. They had behaved in awful fashion, taking every advantage of His goodness and mercy. Finally, He had enough and determined to turn His face away from them, signaling that until they changed their ways and turned back to Him, they no longer had access to Him. In short, for God to hide His face is synonymous with removing His Presence. In fact, He tells them:

> "And many evils and troubles shall befall them, so that they will say in that day, 'Have not these evils come upon us because our God is not among us?'"
>
> – DEUTERONOMY 31:17

Consider the purpose of the Sanctuary. It was not ordained so that there could be a priesthood or offerings. Its primary purpose was that God could dwell among His people.

"Let them make me a sanctuary that I may dwell among them."

– EXODUS 25:8

The Hebrew word that is translated "dwell among," *sh'khanti,* means literally "to dwell inside." The root word, *shakhan,* is where we get the word for "tabernacle," *mishkan,* and the word *shekinah,* which actually means "indwelling presence." Therefore, embedded within the word for Tabernacle is the purpose of the Tabernacle—that He desired to dwell among them as a nation but also within them as individuals.

This speaks to the fact that, from the beginning, God has always wanted to commune with His people. That was the purpose of the Garden, which by the way, was portioned similarly to the Tabernacle. Eden corresponds to the Court. The Garden corresponds to the Holy Place, and the midst of the Garden—where the Tree of Life grew—corresponds to the Holy of Holies.

Again, from the very beginning, God has always wanted to dwell among His people, to be first in their lives, to reign in their hearts and be the object of their love and devotion. Thus it is written that the first and greatest commandment is to "love the Lord your God with all of your heart, soul and strength" (Deut. 6:5). Furthermore, as believers we are admonished to remember:

"Your body is the temple of the Holy Spirit who is in you, whom you have from God, and you are not your own."

– 1 CORINTHIANS 6:19

When God dwells within a person or a nation, there is prosperity, peace and power—not because of the people's merits, but because of the Presence of the Almighty. The ground upon which Moses walked as he approached the burning bush was not created holy; it was made holy by the presence of the Holy One. God's people do not prosper or live in peace solely because of their obedience, but their obedience ensures that the Presence of the Almighty will continue dwelling among them.

"Not by might nor by power, but by My Spirit, says the LORD of hosts."

– ZECHARIAH 4:6

Understanding this, we are prompted to ask the question, "What happens when God's Presence is removed—when He hides His face from His people?" It stands to reason that, if, as the source of life, blessing, peace and prosperity enjoyed by a nation, He were to depart from the nation, then that nation would be stripped of their life, blessing, peace and prosperity.

When considering Israel's history, one disconcerting flaw pops up time and again—they repeatedly began to look around at what all the other nations were doing and desired to be like them in every manner possible. For instance, while in the wilderness they began to recall the food that Egypt had provided for them, disdaining the manna that God had provided for them, and apparently choosing to ignore the bondage they had been under in Egypt.

> "We remember the fish which we ate freely in Egypt, the cucumbers, the melons, the leeks, the onions, and the garlic; but now our whole being is dried up; there is nothing at all except this manna before our eyes!"

– NUMBERS 11:5-6

Their disgruntled attitude and desire for Egyptian fare continued until God determined to give them what they asked for. However, it was to teach them that it was not what they needed. Interestingly, the wind that brought the quail into the camp came from the direction of the Red Sea, in other words, from the direction of Egypt. They got their quail, but at a great price—a plague destroyed thousands of them. The manna from Heaven, a picture of the Word of God and the Messiah, provided life. They chose death.

In another time and another place, the people of Israel once again began to look around at what all the nations had to offer that seemed to be good.

> "Then all the elders of Israel gathered together and came to Samuel at Ramah, and said to him, 'Look, you are old, and your

35

sons do not walk in your ways. Now make us a king to judge
us like all the nations.' But the thing displeased Samuel when
they said, 'Give us a king to judge us.' So Samuel prayed to the
LORD."

– 1 SAMUEL 8:4-6

Again we see that God gave them what they wanted—a king to
judge them like the nations. In the end it didn't turn out so well for
Israel. That king was Saul, son of Kish. As in the wilderness, we see
that God will at times give His people what they want in order to
teach them that what they want is not what they need. Likewise, God
didn't remove the Tree of Knowledge from the midst of the Garden;
He warned the man not to eat of its deadly fruit.

So if God's people are determined to be like the nations, to behave
like the nations and to revere what the nations revere, doesn't it make
sense that they would also reap what the nations reap? If Israel's true
King and His laws no longer inspire them to live according to the covenant and if He no longer appeals to them and their desires because
they have turned away from Him, might He determine to "abdicate"
His Throne—might He hide His face from them?

If His Presence departs from His dwelling place, the people and
the nation, would not the door be left open for another presence
and another king or prince to come in and reside in the now vacated
dwelling place and rule upon the empty throne? The problem for
God's people, however, is that this king, prince or presence does not
have their best interest in mind.

Regarding this issue, Jesus said:

> "When an unclean spirit goes out of a man, he goes through dry
> places, seeking rest, and finds none. Then he says, 'I will return
> to my house from which I came.' And when he comes, he finds it
> empty, swept, and put in order. Then he goes and takes with him
> seven other spirits more wicked than himself, and they enter and
> dwell there; and the last state of that man is worse than the first.
> So shall it also be with this wicked generation."

– MATTHEW 12:43-45

His point is this: The "house" or person that has been delivered of an unclean spirit needs to be filled with the Spirit of God because he is now a temple of the Holy Spirit. However, if the Presence of God is not there—if the house is vacant—the unclean presence, along with other wicked spirits, is free to move in and set up residence. Because Saul would not repent of his pride and continued in his disobedience, God eventually removed His Spirit from the man.

> "But the Spirit of the LORD departed from Saul, and a distressing spirit from the LORD troubled him."
>
> – 1 SAMUEL 16:14

According to Paul the Apostle, at some future time a temple will be built in Jerusalem atop Mount Moriah. However, rather than witnessing the glory of God residing in the Holy of Holies, the world will witness another spectacle:

> "The man of sin ... the son of perdition, who opposes and exalts himself above all that is called God or that is worshiped, so that he sits as God in the temple of God, showing himself that he is God."
>
> – 2 THESSALONIANS 2:3-4

These few passages serve to underscore our previous point: if God's Presence is removed from a person or a nation, another presence—an evil presence—moves in and takes over because God has hidden His face. Thus He said to Israel:

> "And many evils and troubles shall befall them, so that they will say in that day, 'Have not these evils come upon us because our God is not among us?'
>
> – DEUTERONOMY 31:17

Although the "evils and troubles" that would befall Israel may seem to be self-explanatory, because the statement is so general in nature, it could be most anything. Some of what would happen to them is described in Leviticus 26, as we noted before. However, the Hebrew word translated as "troubles" might signify something more specific, and in light of current events, something very compelling.

The word "troubles" in Hebrew is *tzarot* and comes from a root word that means "to squeeze." The idea would be that the "troubles" are intended to squeeze Israel in such a way that they would recognize that God is not among them, and reading between the lines, they would be motivated to repent and return to God. The fascinating aspect about this word is how certain derivatives and family words connect to events going on in today's world, particularly in America.

One derivative of this word, *tzar,* when used as a noun means "an enemy or foe." Believe it or not, the Russian word *tsar* (also *czar,* derived from Caesar, Kaisar) is phonetically related to this word. Another Hebrew family word is *sar* which means "prince." The point would be this: one of the consequences for Israel's abandonment of the covenant was that evils would befall them, as would Cae**sar**s, Kai**sar**s and **tsar**s. In other words, if Israel would not acknowledge the sovereignty of her King, the Almighty, He would remove His Presence and allow another king, tsar or prince to reign in His stead.

While you ponder this interesting connection, it is important to recall that Moses' words were not solely intended for those he spoke to 3,500 years ago. His words were intended to warn us as well.

> "I make this covenant and this oath, not with you alone, but with him who stands here with us today before the LORD our God, as well as with him who is not here with us today."
>
> – DEUTERONOMY 29:14-15

Remembering that to correctly discern the end you must first understand the beginning, the term *tzarot* and its relation to *sar*—"prince"— and *tsar* is incredible. It would seem that future generations of God's people, should they turn from Him and break the covenant, would be subject to evils and troubles—the heavy-handed tyrants of their day, the princes and the tzars. This is because, as we noted earlier, often God will give His people what they want in order to teach them it is not what they need.

CHAPTER FOUR

Lessons from Ancient Israel

*"The farther backward you can look, the
farther forward you are likely to see."*

– WINSTON CHURCHILL

I N AN EFFORT to further accentuate the concept that we are presenting to you, we want to take a look at a couple of key events that transpired in ancient Israel. Interestingly, both of these events involve a Nazirite—in Hebrew, *nazir*. We will begin in 1 Samuel with the birth of the prophet and Nazirite, Samuel.

The story begins with Hannah, the wife of Elkanah, who is unable to conceive. While visiting the tabernacle at Shiloh, she petitions the Lord to give her a male child, who she vows will be His life-long servant and a Nazirite.

> "Then she made a vow and said, 'O LORD of hosts, if You will indeed look on the affliction of Your maidservant and remember me, and not forget Your maidservant, but will give Your maidservant a male child, then I will give him to the LORD all the days of his life, and no razor shall come upon his head.'"
>
> – 1 SAMUEL 1:11

She conceives and delivers a male child, and being true to her vow, takes Samuel back to Shiloh to serve in the Sanctuary and live the life of a Nazirite. This means that all the days of his life Samuel was to abstain from wine and things pertaining to the grape, refrain from touching a corpse and never cut his hair. This is important to remember for reasons we will address soon.

Even as Samuel was growing up in the Sanctuary, Israel was going through very tumultuous and dark times. Specifically, these were the days when the High Priest, Eli, and his wicked sons, Hophni and Phineas, officiated in the tabernacle. Concerning Eli, the Bible says that he had grown old, blind, fat and apparently apathetic in his duties. Not only had he allowed the light of the menorah to grow dim (1 Sam. 3:3), but he failed to restrain his two wicked sons from stealing the LORD'S portions of the sacrifices and from committing fornication in and around the tabernacle. At best, Eli gave them a slap on the wrist.

Where his two sons were concerned, the Bible has this to say of them:

> "Now the sons of Eli were corrupt; they did not know the LORD."
>
> – 1 SAMUEL 2:12

The word "corrupt" is translated from the Hebrew term *b'nai Belial*—"sons of Belial." Paul says that believers in Messiah are not to be yoked with Belial. These men were priests—sons of Aaron—but nevertheless they were yoked to Belial and did not know the LORD. Fully aware of their wicked deeds, all Eli managed to do was chasten them with words alone. Apparently no real action was taken to stop them. In his lecture to them Eli makes this point:

> "No, my sons! For it is not a good report that I hear. You make the LORD's people transgress."
>
> – 1 SAMUEL 2:24

In other words, their sin filtered down among and through the people causing them to sin and to abhor "the offering of the LORD" (1 Sam. 2:17). It would be fair to say that, starting with the priests and down through the rank and file of the nation, Israel had been turning their face away from God, hence the warning sent to Eli.

FULFILLMENT OF THE PROPHECY

"Then a man of God came to Eli and said to him, 'Thus says the Lord: did I not clearly reveal myself to the house of your father when they were in Egypt in Pharaoh's house?...Why do you kick at my sacrifice and my offering which I have commanded in my dwelling place and honor your sons more than me, to make yourselves fat with the best of all the offerings of Israel my people?"

– 1 SAMUEL 2:27, 29

There are a couple of points in this verse that we must note. First of all, God did not go to his sons but directly to the High Priest, Eli. Secondly, he pointed out that Eli had preferred his sons — his wicked sons — over God. This strongly suggests that, despite having spoken to them about their actions, Eli never did anything about their actions. Furthermore, if he preferred his sons over the Almighty, then could we not say that he, as the leader of Israel in some respect, had turned his face away from God? Consequently, his focus being what it was would have negatively affected the entire nation.

Lastly, please notice that he and his sons had made themselves "fat with the best of all the offerings of Israel." This is an important point considering that God had told Israel in Deuteronomy 31:

"When I have brought them to the land flowing with milk and honey... and they have eaten and filled themselves and grown fat, then they will turn to other gods and serve them: and they will provoke me and break my covenant."

– DEUTERONOMY 31:20

It would seem that what God told Moses years before was coming to pass in the days of Eli and Samuel. There is still more to the story:

"Behold, the days are coming that I will cut off your arm and the arm of your father's house, so that there will not be an old man in your house. And you will see an enemy in my dwelling place, despite all the good which God does for Israel."

– 1 SAMUEL 2:31–32

In this verse God pledged to remove Eli and his sons from their position, promising in subsequent verses to raise up a faithful priest in their stead, presumably Samuel. In fact, later during a battle with the Philistines, both Hophni and Phineas were killed. We'll come back to that in a moment. Notice, though, God tells Eli that "an enemy" or "foe" would be seen in God's dwelling place.

Remember, God's dwelling place can be viewed as being the nation of Israel at large, because the purpose of the Sanctuary was so He could "dwell among them." The Sanctuary itself was deemed to be His dwelling place, with the Holy of Holies being the chamber where His Presence actually resided. The point is this: through the prophet, God told Eli and Israel that an enemy would reside in His dwelling place, meaning that an enemy would penetrate the Holy of Holies, and consequently the Sanctuary and the nation.

If an enemy were to do this, it could only mean one thing—God's Presence was no longer there; He had hidden His face from them. Perhaps the most fascinating aspect of this is the Hebrew word used here for "enemy"—it is the word *tzar* (tsar)!

Later, when Israel found themselves at war with the Philistines, an initial battle cost Israel some 4,000 men (1 Samuel 4:2). At this point, someone got the idea that word should be sent to Shiloh to fetch the Ark of the Covenant so that the emblem of God's Presence—His Throne on earth—would deliver them from their enemy and bring victory.

The Bible relates that this was done. The Ark was escorted by the *b'nai Belial*—sons of Belial—Hophni and Phineas. With the Ark's arrival, the camp of Israel was confident of victory and reacted with shouts so loud that the earth shook (1 Sam. 4:5). Surely, with God among them there was no chance of defeat; except it did not work out that way. 30,000 Israelites were killed including Hophni and Phineas, and the Ark of the Covenant—God's Throne on earth and representation of His Presence among them—was taken captive by idolaters and pagans.

When Eli learned of the death of his sons and of the Ark's capture, the Bible says:

> "Then it happened, when he made mention of the ark of God, that Eli fell off the seat backward by the side of the gate; and his neck was broken and he died, for the man was old and heavy."
>
> – 1 SAMUEL 4:18

Upon hearing this news, Phineas' wife went into labor and delivered a son.

> "Now his daughter-in-law, Phinehas' wife, was with child, due to be delivered; and when she heard the news that the ark of God was captured, and that her father-in-law and her husband were dead, she bowed herself and gave birth, for her labor pains came upon her. And about the time of her death the women who stood by her said to her, 'Do not fear, for you have borne a son.' But she did not answer, nor did she regard it. Then she named the child Ichabod, saying, 'The glory has departed from Israel!' because the ark of God had been captured and because of her father-in-law and her husband. And she said, 'The glory has departed from Israel, for the ark of God has been captured.'"
>
> – 1 SAMUEL 4:19-22

The name Ichabod literally means "There is no glory"—and, if no glory, no Presence. On that day long ago, as He had foretold decades before, His people had turned to other gods even though they kept thinking God was with them all along. On that day, as He also foretold, He hid His face from them, removing His Presence and making way for the presence of another to come in and be seen in His dwelling place—His people. Only then did Israel realize God was not with them, that His Presence had departed.

> "They will say in that day, 'Have not these evils come upon us because our God is not among us?' "
>
> – DEUTERONOMY 31:17

SAMSON AND THE COVENANT

We need to point out here that when warning Israel of their future apostasy, God did not threaten to hide His face if they broke His commandments. He said:

43

"They will forsake Me and break My covenant which I have made with them."

— Deuteronomy 31:16

"They will turn to other gods and serve them; and they will provoke Me and break My covenant."

— Deuteronomy 31:20

Twice He warns they will break His covenant and that as a result He will remove His Presence. Could we not conclude then that God does not hide His face because of broken commandments but because of a broken covenant? Though we have pointed out that the two go hand-in-glove, there seems to be a distinction made between them as it relates to God hiding His face.

In other words, how many of us have broken any of God's commandments—whether ignorantly or purposely—and still felt Him compelling us to repent and overcome our weakness? How many of us have known we were struggling in His will and still heard His voice urging us to keep pressing toward the mark? All of us!

Again, when it comes to whether He hides His face from us, it would seem there is a difference between breaking His commandments and breaking His covenant. That is not to suggest that we are excused from obedience and given license to disregard His commandments. To the contrary, continually breaking His commands is how a person or nation ends up breaking His covenant.

In order that we might see this concept more clearly, let us now turn our attention to another story in the Old Testament, one that tells us of another male child ordained from birth to be a life-long Nazirite—Samson.

"Now there was a certain man from Zorah, of the family of the Danites, whose name was Manoah; and his wife was barren and had no children. And the Angel of the LORD appeared to the woman and said to her, 'Indeed now, you are barren and have borne no children, but you shall conceive and bear a son. Now therefore, please be careful not to drink wine or similar drink, and not to eat anything unclean. For behold, you shall conceive and bear a son. And no razor shall come upon his head, for the child shall be a Nazirite to God from the womb; and he shall begin to deliver Israel out of the hand of the Philistines."

– JUDGES 13:2-5

Before we begin to look at our lesson from Samson's life, let us recall the three primary prohibitions given to a Nazirite for the duration of their vow:

- Abstain from wine and similar drink.

- Don't touch a carcass or corpse.

- Don't cut the hair.

If you were to compare the prohibitions placed upon a Nazirite and those placed upon a priest, you will discover they are very similar. For instance, priests were told not to drink wine when they were about to enter the Sanctuary (Lev. 10:9). They were instructed not to touch any dead thing while serving in the Tabernacle (Lev. 21:11-12). These connections suggest that the vows of a Nazirite allowed for those not born from the tribe of Levi to express their desire to go beyond a "courtyard" experience and draw closer to God. The connection doesn't end there; the hair of the Nazirite is the most interesting link to the priests.

> "All the days of the vow of his separation no razor shall come upon his head; until the days are fulfilled for which he separated himself to the LORD, he shall be holy. Then he shall let the locks of the hair of his head grow . . . And the priest shall take the boiled shoulder of the ram, one unleavened cake from the basket, and one unleavened wafer, and put them upon the hands of the Nazirite after he has shaved his consecrated hair."
>
> – NUMBERS 6:5, 19

In the above verses, the word "separation" comes from the root word *nazar*—"to separate" or "distance (one's self)." From this we derive the word *nezer*, which is interpreted in verse 19 as "consecrated hair." Actually, the word "hair" is not present there in the Hebew text but is understood, meaning that the unshorn hair of the Nazirite is the *nezer* or "consecration"—something considered holy unto God. The reason we find this to be of interest is the fact that this is the same word rendered "crown" in the verse below. Referring to Aaron, God told Moses:

> "Then you shall take the garments, put the tunic on Aaron, and the robe of the ephod, the ephod, and the breastplate, and gird him with the intricately woven band of the ephod. You shall put the turban on his head, and put the holy crown on the turban."
>
> – Exodus 29:5-6

That this word *nezer* is used in reference to the crown worn by the High Priest—a crown upon which was engraved the words *kadosh l'YHVH*, "Holy unto the LORD"—as well as in reference to the consecrated hair of the Nazirite—also considered holy unto the LORD—is not only interesting, but ties the story of Samson to the story of Samuel and of the High Priest, Eli.

First though, how did Samson do when it came to keeping the instructions relevant to the vow (covenant) of the Nazirite? In the matter of wine and similar drink, did he keep that commandment? Frankly, we can't be certain for the Bible doesn't say specifically one way or the other. We do know that he, on occasion, visited harlots (Judges 16:1), that he had a desire for strange women who often enticed him and that he celebrated at a wedding feast with his Philistine wife. We are left to speculate, but considering all of his other indiscretions, it's not hard to imagine that, at some point, he may have had a glass of wine or two.

When it comes to the second prohibition, we don't have to speculate at all. At least on two occasions we know that Samson touched something dead or pertaining to a carcass. First, there was the honey that he retrieved from the lion he had previously killed (Judges 14:8-9). Then there was the time he used the jawbone of a donkey to kill 1,000 men.

> "When he came to Lehi, the Philistines came shouting against him. Then the Spirit of the LORD came mightily upon him; and

the ropes that were on his arms became like flax that is burned with fire, and his bonds broke loose from his hands. He found a fresh jawbone of a donkey, reached out his hand and took it, and killed a thousand men with it. Then Samson said: 'With the jawbone of a donkey, heaps upon heaps, with the jawbone of a donkey I have slain a thousand men!'"

– JUDGES 15:14-16

Obviously the donkey was dead, meaning Samson touched something that was forbidden to him. Yet at the same time, the Bible clearly states that the "Spirit of the LORD came mightily upon him." The point is, even though Samson broke certain commandments, the Spirit of God would still come upon him. Does that mean we can ignore God's commands and do as we will? Absolutely not. It is just to demonstrate, once again, that God does not hide His face from His people simply because of a broken commandment. It takes much more than that.

As the story proceeds and Samson involves himself with the Philistine Delilah, something much more tragic occurs. He reveals the source of his strength—his consecrated hair or *nezer*. As we all know, foolishly, Samson eventually relented to Delilah's persistent inquiries to know the source of his strength. Finally, as he lay in her lap sleeping, the hair—the consecrated hair—was shorn from his head, and heaven only knows what became of it. It was supposed to be "holy unto the LORD" but instead became the property of uncircumcised Philistines. At this point, Delilah said:

> "The Philistines are upon you, Samson!" So he awoke from his sleep, and said, 'I will go out as before, at other times, and shake myself free!' But he did not know that the LORD had departed from him."

– JUDGES 16:20

Up until this point, even though he had often broken God's commands, the Spirit of God would still come upon him. So what made this time different? By allowing his *nezer*—consecrated hair—to be shorn and profaned by idolaters, it was as if the High Priest of Israel had taken the crown inscribed with "Holy unto the LORD" and cast it to dogs. In some ways, it could be likened to what Eli did with his crown. In effect, he defiled it by allowing his sons to continue in their wickedness.

The difference this time was that, beyond breaking a command, Samson had broken the covenant. As a result, Samson discovered too late that God had hidden His face from Him. His Presence was no longer with him, which allowed another presence to overpower him and put out his eyes.

COME LET US RETURN

> "In that day the deaf shall hear the words of the book, and the eyes of the blind shall see out of obscurity and out of darkness."
>
> – ISAIAH 29:18

If there is a silver lining to this tragedy and the one at Shiloh, it is that sometimes you have to be blinded in order to see. Sometimes you have to lose something in order to be motivated to find it. Samson was blinded, but in that darkness he began to look and to seek—as his consecrated hair began to grow back. Saul of Tarsus lost his sight long enough to "see" that Jesus was the promised Messiah (Acts 9:17-18).

Even though the presumed destruction of the Tabernacle at Shiloh and the loss of the Ark of the Covenant were tragic events, not to mention the death of the High Priest, God already had someone ready to step in and lead Israel—Samuel. Furthermore, even though He did allow these evils and troubles to befall the nation, it was not intended for their destruction, but so they would be provoked to repentance. You see, not only did He foretell of their great apostasy, but also of a time when they would begin to seek that which they had lost.

> "And the LORD will scatter you among the peoples, and you will be left few in number among the nations where the LORD will drive you. And there you will serve gods, the work of men's hands, wood and stone, which neither see nor hear nor eat nor smell. But from there you will seek the LORD your God, and you will find Him if you seek Him with all your heart and with all your soul. When you are in distress, and all these things come

upon you in the latter days, when you turn to the LORD your God and obey His voice (for the LORD your God is a merciful God), He will not forsake you nor destroy you, nor forget the covenant of your fathers which He swore to them."

— DEUTERONOMY 4:27-31

Here it is made clear that there would come a day when His people, though scattered among the nations, would begin to seek Him and would find Him IF they searched with ALL of their heart. Perhaps that is to suggest that, instead of fixing their gaze upon those other gods, they would begin to turn their face back to the One and only God. Also, this turning back to Him would occur when they were in "distress"—the Hebrew word being, *tzar*—and would be in the latter days. This same concept is echoed by the prophet when, writing of backslidden Israel, he says:

> "Come, and let us return to the LORD; for He has torn, but He will heal us; He has stricken, but He will bind us up. After two days He will revive us; on the third day He will raise us up, that we may live in His sight."

— HOSEA 6:1-2

Thus the remedy is for God's people to turn back to Him, to seek His face by turning their face back to Him. When they do, notice what happens. They will live in His sight, hinting that He has turned His face back toward them. You see, even though He hid His face, it was only for a season.

> "When I have brought them back from the peoples and gathered them out of their enemies' lands, and I am hallowed in them in the sight of many nations, then they shall know that I am the LORD their God, who sent them into captivity among the nations, but also brought them back to their land, and left none of them captive any longer. And I will not hide My face from them anymore; for I shall have poured out My Spirit on the house of Israel,' says the Lord GOD."

— EZEKIEL 39:27-29

Remember the mother who turned her back to her child? Imagine that the child finally realizes that it is his actions that have brought about being "cut off" from his mother. What if the child apologizes for his misdeeds and asks for his mother's forgiveness? Would she not gladly turn her face back to the child and, once again, give him access to her care and her love? Though God forsook them for a season, He also said to them:

> "He will not forsake you nor destroy you, nor forget the covenant of your fathers..."
>
> – DEUTERONOMY 4:31

Like the Prodigal who came to his senses and determined to return to his father's house — to set his face toward his father, seeking his face — so may it be also with God's wayward sons and daughters (Lk. 15:11-32). May we all turn our face back to Him that He will be provoked to turn His face back toward us as the Priestly Benediction declares:

> "The LORD bless you and keep you; the LORD make His face shine upon you, and be gracious to you; the LORD lift up His countenance upon you, and give you peace."
>
> – NUMBERS 6:24-26

A LESSON FOR AMERICA

What happened to Samson and what happened at Shiloh demonstrates what will happen to a nation that, though once in relationship with God, decides to turn away from God and embrace worthless things and biblically-foreign philosophies. Their "other gods" may not be idols of wood and stone, but they don't have to be. They can be anything that becomes more important than their commitment to the covenant made with the Almighty. In our opinion, such is the state of affairs in America today.

So then, the real purpose for reciting all of this pertinent information regarding the covenant and the consequences for breaking covenant is to underscore the question we posed in the introduction — why is the West faltering and, specifically, why is the United States coming apart at the seams? It should be obvious by now, but in case you missed it, here it is. We are suggesting that America has, like Eli, Hophni, Phineas, Samson and Israel, gone beyond breaking God's command-ments and has unfortunately broken His covenant.

Sadly, every indication is that He is beginning to "hide His face" from this nation. May we return to Him before it is too late and we realize that evils and troubles have come upon us because "our God is not among us."

CHAPTER FIVE

America's Covenant with the God of Israel

"The teachings of the Bible are so interwoven and entwined with our whole civic and social life that it would be literally—I do not mean figuratively, I mean literally—impossible for us to figure to ourselves what life would be if these teachings were removed."

– THEODORE ROOSEVELT

T HROUGHOUT THE CONSTITUTIONAL Convention of 1787, the deliberations were held in strict secrecy. Consequently, anxious citizens gathered outside of Independence Hall in Philadelphia when the proceedings ended in order to learn of the outcome. It has been handed down to us that a Mrs. Powell of Philadelphia asked Benjamin Franklin, "Well, Doctor, what have we got, a republic or a monarchy?" Quickly, Franklin responded, "A republic, if you can keep it."

What did he mean by his response "if you can keep it"? Did this betray a bit of uncertainty on his part? Perhaps he doubted that the American people would uphold and preserve the Constitution and be true to the Biblical and moral principles upon which it was based. Now almost 230 years later, in consideration of the national state of affairs, the statement by Franklin prompts the question, "Have we kept it?" Have we held on to the principles that shaped our republic, or have we allowed what was entrusted to us to slip from our grasp and devolve into what the Founders abhorred and feared—a democracy, mob rule, or even worse, outright lawlessness and the tyranny that is sure to follow?

More importantly, have we turned our face away from the One who inspired and guided the founders of this nation, who time and again intervened to preserve and sustain her? Have we forsaken the One who blessed us beyond what those early pioneers and Puritan preachers could have ever imagined? Have we provoked Him to hide His face from us?

Before we delve too far into that issue, let's look at some of the highlights of our national heritage so that we might better understand who and what our Founders were and, most importantly, what they believed about the God of Israel and His Word. Furthermore, we want to know whether or not they considered themselves to be in covenant with Him, both as individuals and as a nation.

POTENT QUOTES

First of all, we must acknowledge that time and space precludes us from listing and quoting even a small fraction of the material available which supports the argument that this nation was founded, settled and developed by people who believed in, prayed to and strove to faithfully serve the God of Israel. Consider that when over 15,000 quotes obtained from various papers, articles and books attributed to the Framers and Founders were evaluated, the results showed that 35% of these quotes were taken directly from or inspired by the Bible.

Still, in order to establish that God did, in fact, ordain and call into being this nation and that those early pioneers, pastors, and, yes, politicians understood that to be true, we will offer you a sampling of these quotes.

Even before there was an America, the man credited with discovering the New World, Christopher Columbus, viewed himself as a "servant ... of the Most High Savior, Christ." Queen Isabella of Spain characterized his voyage as an expedition to "bear the light of Christ west to the heathen undiscovered lands."

Over a century later, English explorers and investors established the first permanent British colony on the banks of the James River, dubbing their settlement "Jamestown." Admittedly, this was predominantly a failed business venture, nevertheless, King James himself wrote in the preamble of the Virginia Company's Charter his view of their venture — "propagating of Christian religion to such people as yet live in darkness and ignorance of the true knowledge and worship of God."

When the Mayflower landed at Cape Cod in November 1620, those aboard felt it prudent to draft a document that would state their purpose for establishing a colony and serve as a governmental document, binding all those who ratified it to exist under the rule of laws mutually agreed to. This "one law, one people" concept is something taken directly from Scripture.

> "You shall have the same law for the stranger and for one from your own country; for I am the LORD your God."
>
> — LEVITICUS 24:22

Thus the Mayflower Compact, signed on November 11, 1620, became America's first governmental document—one inspired by the greatest of all documents—and, therefore, merits mentioning here. A portion of it reads (in an updated English version):

> "We whose names are underwritten, loyal subjects of our dread sovereign Lord, King James...have undertaken, for the glory of God and advancement of the Christian faith and honor of our King and country, a voyage to plant the first colony in the northern parts of Virginia, do by these present solemnly and mutually, in the presence of God and of one another, covenant and combine ourselves together into a civil body politic, for our better ordering and preservation and furtherance of the ends aforesaid..."

According to their own testimony, their stated purpose was, first and foremost, to plant a colony for the "glory of God" and to advance "the Christian faith." In so doing, they determined to covenant with one another in the "presence of God" to bring this about. It is apparent that these men and women understood the sanctity of a covenant, respecting its responsibility as well as valuing its reward.

And it is these brave people—many of them nameless in the annals of history—who, in conjunction with the Puritans of the Massachusetts Bay Colony, had as much as anyone to do with what would become the United States. Men like Washington, Revere, Hancock and Adams—though invaluable to the American saga—all followed in the footsteps of these determined sojourners who came here to live in covenant with God and their fellow man.

In 1647, William Bradford, governor of Plymouth, said of his fellow colonists in his famous work, *Of Plymouth Plantation*:

> "Last and not least, they cherished a great hope and inward zeal of laying the foundations, or at least making some ways toward it, for the propagation and advance of the gospel of the kingdom of Christ in the remote parts of the world, even though they should be but stepping stones to others in the performance of so great a work....Thus out of small beginnings greater things have been produced by His hand that made all things of nothing, and gives being to all things that are;...Let the glorious name of Jehovah have all the praise."

It is abundantly clear that the inhabitants of Plymouth Plantation viewed themselves as being in covenant with one another and with God. They also saw themselves as laying the foundation for something greater than their small, humble settlement. It is reminiscent in some fashion of the story of Abraham, who:

> "By faith ... obeyed when he was called to go out to the place which he would receive as an inheritance. And he went out, not knowing where he was going. By faith he dwelt in the land of promise as in a foreign country, dwelling in tents with Isaac and Jacob, the heirs with him of the same promise; for he waited for the city which has foundations, whose builder and maker is God....These all died in faith, not having received the promises, but having seen them afar off were assured of them, embraced them and confessed that they were strangers and pilgrims on the earth. For those who say such things declare plainly that they seek a homeland."

> – HEBREWS 11:8-10, 13-14

If they perceived their efforts in Massachusetts to be part of a larger plan designed by the Great Architect, they also understood that success would require that their energies be spent on spiritual objectives as much, if not more so, as on building fences, homes and roads. If we may phrase it this way: they committed themselves to live according to the essential elements of the covenant demonstrated in the Scripture, ratified by the blood of Messiah—"Love the LORD your God with all your heart" and "Love your neighbor as yourself." This would bring them prosperity.

Others would pick up where they left off. A century and a half later their descendants would fire the first shots of the Revolution. Joining them would be other notable men from other regions of the continent who would spur on the citizens of America to establish a nation based on Biblical principle, faith in God and a covenantal relationship with the Almighty and one another. They made their goal clear: to establish a nation like no other since the days of King David; one "conceived in liberty, and dedicated to the proposition that all men are created equal."

And so it was that in 1787, Benjamin Franklin and other statesmen, as well as clergymen, gave birth to the Republic and produced the U.S. Constitution—a document whose forerunners and inspiration included the Mayflower Compact and other biblically inspired works—in an effort to "insure the blessings of liberty to ourselves and our posterity."

It cannot be understated that the Constitution, our national covenant with God and one another, has a direct link to the Law of Moses, God's covenantal contract with Israel. Many, including presidents, agree on this point. One hundred sixty years after its adoption, one of them, President Harry S. Truman, would say:

> "The fundamental basis of this nation's laws was given to Moses on the Mount. The fundamental basis of our Bill of Rights comes from the teachings we get from Exodus and Matthew, from Isaiah and Paul. I don't think we emphasize that enough these days. If we don't have a proper fundamental moral background,

we will finally end up with a totalitarian government which does
not believe in rights for anybody except the state."

American history is saturated with evidence to support the notion
that our forefathers understood that it was the God of Israel, and no
other, who directed their paths, orchestrated history and established
the new nation. History also reveals to us how they viewed the future
of the nation and what would be required in order for America to
prosper and be sustained. Time and again, they stressed that the
American people must remain faithful to the Biblical principles that
birthed the nation and that granted them unparalleled blessing.

In 1788, after the ratification of the Constitution, George
Washington wrote to his deputy, Benjamin Lincoln:

> "No country upon the earth ever had it more in its power to
> attain these blessings.... Much to be regretted indeed would it
> be, were we to neglect the means and depart from the road which
> Providence has pointed us to, so plainly; I cannot believe it will
> ever come to pass. The Great Governor of the Universe has led us
> too long and too far ... to forsake us in the midst of it ... We may,
> now and then, get bewildered; but I hope and trust that there is
> good sense and virtue enough left to recover the right path."

Seventy-five years later, another Lincoln would recall the noble
effort to establish such a nation "under God." On the battlefield
of Gettysburg he would also invoke the memory of those who had
given their life's blood in order to ensure that the "government of the
people, by the people, for the people shall not perish from the earth."
Considering Lincoln's famous observation and that of Washington in
regard to America's future, it is obvious that they also understood the
responsibility that must be lived up to in order for the nation to continue. In other words, they perceived the national danger of forsaking
God and His covenant.

Many years before Gettysburg, Yorktown or Valley Forge, and even
before there was a place called Boston or Philadelphia, a Puritan pastor,
later governor of Massachusetts Bay, by the name of John Winthrop
sat on the deck of the ship, *Arbella*, and authored his famous work, *A*

Model of Christian Charity. As he journeyed to the New World, he wrote these poignant and sobering words:

> "We are a company, professing ourselves fellow members of Christ, and thus we ought to account ourselves knit together by this bond of love.... Thus stands the cause between God and us: we are entered into covenant with Him for this work. We have taken out a commission; the Lord hath given us leave to draw our own articles.

> If the Lord shall please to hear us, and bring us in peace to the place we desire, then hath He ratified this Covenant and sealed our commission, and will expect a strict performance of the Articles.... The Lord will surely break out in wrath against us. Now the only way to avoid this shipwreck and to provide for our posterity is to follow the counsel of Micah: to do justly, to love mercy, to walk humbly with our God. For this end, we must be knit together in this work as one man.

> We shall find that the God of Israel is among us, when ten of us shall be able to resist a thousand of our enemies, when He shall make us a praise and glory, that men of succeeding plantations shall say, 'The Lord make it like that of New England.' We must consider that we shall be as a City upon a Hill, the eyes of all people are upon us; so that if we shall deal falsely with our God in this work we have undertaken and so cause Him to withdraw His present help from us, we shall be made a story and a by-word through the world."

Now, closely consider these words. Winthrop leaves no doubt as to how these people approached the issue of establishing settlements in the New World. If they were to succeed, they MUST be in covenant with God and each other. Furthermore, they understood that this covenant required them to be faithful to Him, His Word and to the virtue of brotherly love. To fail in this commitment — to break this covenant — would "cause Him to withdraw His present help" and would result in despairing consequences.

Understanding that this model—"Love the LORD your God" and "Love your neighbor as yourself"—became the preferred model for other colonies; knowing that this type of devotion is what inspired future generations to fight at Lexington-Concord and other battle-fields, and recognizing that others would call upon the wisdom of Winthrop, Bradford and others to guide them as they established the United States, how can anyone deny that these pioneers and founders were committed to a covenant with God? Furthermore, if they committed to this covenant as a nation, then as a nation, we suffer the consequences if we fail to live up to it.

At this point, maybe you're thinking that in no way should He or would He hold us accountable for what they believed 400 years ago. Is it ridiculous for us to think that their perception was based in reality or that what they thought mattered to God? Could their acknowledgment of a covenant have such far-reaching consequences? Even if they looked at it that way, could it not be that they were just a bunch of religious zealots and that God didn't view it that way at all? We would respond to such objections and questions with one of our own. When Hannah vowed that her unborn son, Samuel, would be God's lifelong servant and Nazirite, did God acknowledge and honor that vow even though Samuel had nothing to do with making the vow? Did He not expect Samuel to be true to it anyway?

Likewise, when it was told to Samson's mother before his birth that he was to be a lifelong Nazirite, was not Samson expected to be faithful to it, and did he not pay the price for breaking it? To be sure, feigning ignorance to the terms of a covenant and failing to uphold its tenets is dangerous to an individual or to a nation. To think that America didn't covenant with God is to ignore and refute what countless men and women have testified of for over two centuries.

"We have staked the whole future of American civilization, not upon the power of government, far from it. We have staked the future of all our political institutions upon the capacity of mankind for self-government; upon the capacity of each and all of us to govern ourselves, to control ourselves, to sustain ourselves according to the Ten Commandments of God."

– JAMES MADISON

This precept—not American ingenuity and know-how—is why "God shed His grace on thee" and why we have enjoyed peace, prosperity and power. Based on what we have inherited and heretofore enjoyed, it would seem that He, as Winthrop put it, "ratified this covenant and sealed our commission." We may have forgotten the covenant made by our forefathers, but He has not!

AMERICA'S PATTERNS WITH ANCIENT ISRAEL

For years now, you have heard us comment upon the distinct and specific parallels between the United States and the nation of Israel. From the time that Columbus' expedition first spotted land on the last, great day of Sukkot (Feast of Tabernacles), to the founding of Jamestown on May 14, 1607, (the modern state of Israel being reborn on May 14, 1948), the early exploration and settlement of the New World was laced with Hebraic themes. It didn't end there.

When Salem, Massachusetts, was established in 1628, it was settled by men who were part of the so-called Great Migration from England to New England, or what the Puritans considered to be an Exodus from Egypt to the Promised Land. Consequently, many of them regarded themselves as neo-Israelites journeying to Canaan to establish a new commonwealth of and for God's people. In this spirit, they called their first settlement, Salem, after the original Salem which later became Jerusalem.

This fascination and connection to ancient Israel permeated the colonies of New England to the degree that laws were based on Mosaic statutes. The Hebrew language was studied, taught, and if some had had their way, would have become the accepted language of the colonies. One of those early founders who adored the language of the Bible was none other than Governor William Bradford of Plymouth Plantation. He wrote:

> "Though I am grown aged, yet I have had a longing desire, to see with my own eyes something of the most ancient language and holy tongue, in which the Law and oracles of God were writ(ten); and in which God and angels spoke to the holy patriarchs, of old time, and what names were given to things, from the Creation."

When Bradford was laid to rest at Burial Hill in Plymouth, MA, a marker was engraved with these words:

> "Under this stone rests…William Bradford, a zealous Puritan and sincere Christian Governor of Plymouth Colony…"

Beneath that inscription is one written in Latin which, translated, says:

> "What our fathers with so much difficulty attained, do not basely relinquish."

Above that is the phrase, written in Hebrew:

> "Yahweh is the Help/Strength of my Life."

Over a century later in April 1775, the "shot heard 'round the world" was fired at the Old North Bridge just outside of Concord, Massachusetts, not too far from Plymouth. The farmers and minutemen who comprised the different militia of the region were the descendants of those who had come to New England and settled places like Salem, Lincoln, Boston, Lexington and Concord. These were the sons of Winthrop, Mather, Edwards and Bradford. When they returned fire at the British Regulars that morning, April 19, 1775, they initiated a struggle that would last for years but, in the end, would liberate them from the greatest military power on the face of the earth.

Interestingly, that day fell during the festival of Unleavened Bread, a season inaugurated with the eating of the Passover, indicating that America's struggle for freedom began at the same time on the Hebrew calendar as did Israel's liberation from Egypt, the most powerful nation of their time. Years later, either because of coincidence or because they were aware of this unique circumstance, Benjamin Franklin and Thomas Jefferson proposed that the Seal of the United States should depict the children of Israel crossing the Red Sea while being pursued by Pharaoh. Beneath this scene were the words, "Rebellion to Tyrants is Obedience to God." It was rejected in favor of the present seal, nevertheless, here again we see the founders of the nation identifying with ancient Israel.

In an interesting footnote to this American-Israeli connection, the United States is referred to in Hebrew as *artzot ha'brit*—"land of the covenant"; a concept that was accentuated with the ratification of the Constitution and the creation of a federal government. The word *federal* comes from the Latin word *foedus* and means, "of or from a compact, agreement or covenant." That Latin word is, in turn, related to another Latin word, *fides,* which is interpreted as "faith."

It is our strong opinion that no other single nation can lay claim to such a strong connection to the Israel of the Bible, and most importantly, know beyond any doubt that it was the God of Israel who planted the seeds that grew that nation. With all due respect to our friends and brethren in other nations, America has such a distinction. However, along with that unique status and the blessings that have been bestowed upon us also comes the responsibility to uphold it and the consequences if we do not. Now, if that connection is valid we must ask, "What was and what is God's purpose for America?

GOD'S PURPOSE FOR THE REPUBLIC

"Now let me sing to my well-beloved a song of my beloved regarding His vineyard: my well-beloved has a vineyard on a very fruitful hill. He dug it up and cleared out its stones, and planted it with the choicest vine. He built a tower in its midst, and also made a winepress in it; so He expected it to bring forth good grapes, but it brought forth wild grapes.... And now, please let Me tell you what I will do to My vineyard: I will take away its hedge, and it shall be burned; and break down its wall, and it shall be trampled down. I will lay it waste; it shall not be pruned or dug, but there shall come up briers and thorns. I will also command the clouds that they rain no rain on it. The vineyard of the LORD of hosts is the house of Israel and the men of Judah are His pleasant plant. He looked for justice, but behold, oppression; for righteousness, but behold, a cry for help."

– ISAIAH 5:1-2 & 5-6

Just as He warned them in Deuteronomy 31, God continued to warn Israel of the consequences of her backslidden ways. Like a vineyard once tended with the utmost care, producing bad fruit prompted the owner of the vineyard to allow it to be burned and laid waste. Naturally, this is not what He had intended. He wanted the vineyard to produce good fruit so that He and, presumably, others could enjoy its bounty.

This is exactly what God had intended for Israel. This was their purpose—to produce the fruit of righteousness for their sake and the sake of others. They were to be the oracles of God and a light to the Gentiles, that those in darkness would be drawn to that light. Unfortunately for the nations and for Israel, God's people failed to produce the proper fruit, instead rendering "wild grapes."

What does this have to do with America? Remember, we have that unique connection with Israel, so in some ways, those principles, blessings, responsibilities and **warnings** that were given to Israel apply to us—that is, if we have chosen to identify with the God of Israel and His Word. So, if Israel is His vineyard, and if America identifies so uniquely with Israel and the God of Israel, how might this vineyard analogy relate to us? Let us look to another parable, one given by Christ in the Gospel of Matthew.

> "Hear another parable: There was a certain landowner who planted a vineyard and set a hedge around it, dug a winepress in it and built a tower. And he leased it to vinedressers and went into a far country. Now when vintage-time drew near, he sent his servants to the vinedressers, that they might receive its fruit. And the vinedressers took his servants, beat one, killed one, and stoned another. Again he sent other servants, more than the first, and they did likewise to them. Then last of all he sent his son to them, saying, 'They will respect my son.' But when the vinedressers saw the son, they said among themselves, 'This is the heir. Come, let us kill him and seize his inheritance.' So they took him and cast him out of the vineyard and killed him. Therefore, when the owner of the vineyard comes, what will he do to those vinedressers?"
>
> – MATTHEW 21:33-40

First of all, notice the similarities between this parable and that of Isaiah 5. It is likely that Jesus knew His listeners would be quick to connect His parable with Isaiah's, thus they would have known that He was speaking of Israel and the men of Judah. Secondly, the vine-dressers leased the vineyard, meaning they did not own it; someone else did, and at vintage He expected to receive good fruit. Finally, in this parable the owner's son was killed by the men who were leasing the vineyard so that they might seize the property for themselves.

Clearly, Jesus intended for His listeners to understand that He was the Son, and that they would do this to Him. Consequently, He posed the question, "What do you think will happen to these men?"

> "They said to Him, 'He will destroy those wicked men miserably, and lease his vineyard to other vinedressers who will render to him the fruits in their seasons.' ... Therefore I say to you, the kingdom of God will be taken from you and given to a nation bearing the fruits of it. And whoever falls on this stone will be broken; but on whomever it falls, it will grind him to powder. Now when the chief priests and Pharisees heard His parables, they perceived that He was speaking of them."
>
> – MATTHEW 21:41, 43-45

In a manner of speaking, Messiah's reply to their answer was, "You're right in everything you just said." What did they say?

- The vineyard would be taken from them.

- They would be destroyed.

- The vineyard would be leased to others and produce fruit.

In case there were any doubts as to exactly what He was inferring, He made sure they knew He was speaking of them, and that the vineyard—the Kingdom of God—would be taken from them. Though they would be destroyed, the vineyard would go on. It would be given to a "nation" whose sole purpose for existence would be to bear fruit.

The question then becomes, "Who and where is this nation Christ referred to?"

It would be safe to say that, first and foremost, this nation is the Body of Christ which is present in every nation on earth and comprised of every ethnicity, nationality and tongue. It knows no political or natural boundaries, because the "earth is the LORD's and the fullness thereof." Still, is it possible that in addition to this, Christ hints at the fact that there would be a country, perhaps even an eclectic mixture of people from all over the world, that would be birthed for the exclusive purpose of bearing the fruits of the Kingdom?

God does, indeed, raise up nations and kings for His purposes. Whether they be a Cyrus who will facilitate the rebuilding of Jerusalem or a Nebuchadnezzar who will destroy Jerusalem, God is the one who ordains the rise and fall of nations.

> "For the kingdom is the LORD's, and He rules over the nations."
>
> – PSALM 22:28

> "God reigns over the nations; God sits on His holy throne."
>
> – PSALM 47:8

> "Yes, all kings shall fall down before Him; all nations shall serve Him."
>
> – PSALM 72:11

> "All nations whom You have made shall come and worship before You, O Lord, and shall glorify Your name."
>
> – PSALM 86:9

Eventually, America was raised up in order to serve His purpose. And, as history records, those men and women He chose to bring about His purpose understood their mission—to be a light among and to the nations and produce the righteous fruit of His vineyard.

When Columbus' expedition sighted land on October 12, 1492—on the last day of the Feast of Tabernacles—among his crew were several Jews; one of them reportedly the man credited with first sighting land, Rodrigo de Triana. This is important because the possibility, if not probability, exists that at least one of them, maybe even de

Triana, may have practiced his religion. If so, one of the prayers for that day, Hoshana Rabbah, would have included this fascinating petition to Heaven:

> "As Thou didst save ... the people singled out for God's salvation—so save Thou us! ... They passed between the deep divided sea; and with them for their guide, the light from Thee—so save Thou us! ... Establish us as Thy *chosen vineyard* and make us as a tree planted by the streams of water ... plant us, we pray, upon a fruitful sod."

It was also on that day that Columbus, stepping onto the sandy beach and planting the standard of Ferdinand and Isabella, reportedly prayed:

> "O Lord, Almighty and Everlasting God, by Thy Holy Word Thou hast created the Heaven and the earth and the sea; blessed and glorified be Thy Name, and praised be Thy Majesty, which hath deigned to use us, Thy humble servants, that Thy holy Name may be proclaimed in this second part of the earth."

Say what you will about these men. Imperfect though they were, they nevertheless acknowledged that, in spite of their imperfections, the Almighty had chosen them to bring about His purposes. Thus, was the beginning of what would eventually become the United States. Others would echo an acknowledgment of being servants in a plan larger than they; one designed to advance God's Kingdom and bring about the fulfillment of His Word.

One such acknowledgement came from a former president and son of a former president, John Quincy Adams, who on July 4, 1837, as Representative Adams, addressed a crowd of celebrants gathered to celebrate the 61st anniversary of the signing of the Declaration of Independence. In what some might regard as patriotic hyperbole, but what we regard as his genuine assessment of America's spiritual impact, Adams spoke of the importance of the day:

> "Is it not that, in the chain of human events, the birthday of the nation is indissolubly linked with the birth of the Savior? That it forms a leading event in the progress of the Gospel dispensation?

Is it not that the Declaration of Independence first organized the social compact on the foundation of the Redeemer's mission upon the earth? That it laid the cornerstone of human government upon the first precepts of Christianity and gave to the world the first irrevocable pledge of the fulfillment of the prophecies announced directly from Heaven at the birth of the Savior and predicted by the greatest of the Hebrew prophets 600 years before?"

Who can argue the fact that America did become the greatest power and most blessed nation on the face of the earth, at least in the modern era? Furthermore, what other one nation has done more to advance the Gospel, to feed the poor and help the widow and fatherless, here and abroad?

Notwithstanding, America has had and continues to have her problems. America and her citizens have never been completely righteous. We have always had corruption, violence, indecency and every type of wickedness that may be found in any culture. Still, who can deny that in spite of these warts and flaws, God has used this nation to be a stabilizing force in the world and one that, with some exceptions, has been a beacon of light rather than darkness?

Let us put it this way: America has been like Samson, who certainly displayed his weaknesses and often broke God's commandments, but was, nevertheless, used by God to defeat Israel's enemies. In fact, when Samson first went to take a wife from among the Philistines—something he was not supposed to do—the Bible says:

"Then his father and mother said to him, 'Is there no woman among the daughters of your brethren, or among all my people, that you must go and get a wife from the uncircumcised Philistines?' And Samson said to his father, 'Get her for me, for she pleases me well.' But his father and mother did not know that it was of the LORD—that He was seeking an occasion to move against the Philistines. For at that time the Philistines had dominion over Israel."

– Judges 14:3-4

Incidents such as this may aggravate our theology, but the fact remains that God uses whom He will for whatever He wills. This includes nations who, more often than not, come up short where His commandments are concerned. However, just like Samson—who eventually broke the covenant—nations who turn from God and break His covenant must endure the dire consequences of forgetting, forsaking and abandoning the covenant once widely and whole-heartedly embraced. Just like Samson, there will come a day when they will go out to face their enemy saying, "I will go out as before, at other times, and shake myself free," and not realize that the LORD has departed from them.

There is an interesting story concerning Abraham Lincoln's first inauguration and the Bible he used to take the oath of office. Lincoln was elected in one of the most volatile and dangerous times in American history—the nation was about to break apart. Because threats had been made against him by Southern sympathizers, Lincoln had to enter Washington under heavy guard and unannounced. Consequently, his belongings, including his Bible, had not arrived by the time of the swearing-in ceremony. As the story goes, a clerk of the Supreme Court fetched a Bible that he used for official purposes, and this was the one on which Lincoln placed his hand as he took the oath of office on March 4, 1861. It would come to be known as the "Lincoln Bible."

The Bible was initially retained and kept by the Court clerk, but at some unknown time, the Lincolns acquired it from him. The Bible remained with the Lincoln family until 1928, at which point Mary Eunice Harlan, the wife of Robert Todd Lincoln, donated it to the Library of Congress. When the Bible was examined, markers were found in two places—Hosea 4 and Deuteronomy 31! As one reads these two chapters, it is quiet easy to spot the common theme: God's people played the harlot and forsook Him and His Word. As a result, He will hide His face from them allowing for destruction and desolation.

"Hear the word of the LORD, You children of Israel, for the LORD brings a charge against the inhabitants of the land: There is no truth or mercy or knowledge of God in the land. ...Therefore the land will mourn; and everyone who dwells there will waste away.... My people are destroyed for lack of knowledge. Because you have rejected knowledge, I also will reject you from being priest for Me; because you have forgotten the law of your God, I also will forget your children. ... Their drink is rebellion, they commit harlotry continually. Her rulers dearly love dishonor."

– HOSEA 4:1, 3, 6, 18

"Then My anger shall be aroused against them in that day, and I will forsake them, and I will hide My face from them, and they shall be devoured. And many evils and troubles shall befall them, so that they will say in that day, 'Have not these evils come upon us because our God is not among us?' And I will surely hide My face in that day because of all the evil which they have done, in that they have turned to other gods."

– DEUTERONOMY 31:17-18

Coincidence or not, it bears noting that it was the "Lincoln Bible" that Barack Obama chose to place his hand upon when he took the oath of office at his 2009 and 2013 inaugurations.

CHAPTER SIX

A Time for Change

*"It's been a long time coming, but tonight, because
of what we did on this day, in this election, at this
defining moment, change has come to America."*

– BARACK OBAMA, NOV. 4, 2008

E VERY NATION GOES through it; in the midst of their development, which may be hundreds of years, they experience an
internal crisis and desire to seek a change. What that change
ends up looking like depends on the character of the people. More
often than not, it occurs when that nation, for some unexplained
reason, loses touch with their history, their heritage, their culture, and
in Israel's case, their God.

The past is forgotten, ignored and eventually redefined. *Change*
compels them to look forward, not backward. Advocates for *change*
preach that hope and light are in the future, not in the dismal recesses
of the past. When *change* is presented to the masses, it is made to
sound noble, inspirational and good; however, the evil component is
never mentioned. You see, *change*, as man defines it, is synonymous
with evolutionary thinking. We want change, so we can evolve into
something better, or so we think.

The glaring problem with this line of thinking is that, from a biblical point of view, it ignores the established record of the past and
rewrites history. So then, if reality happens to get in the way, reality

is redefined; if established law blocks the path, we ignore, erase and replace the law with something that accommodates the change. Another major problem with this line of thinking is that, at least for those nations who have entered into covenant with the God of Israel, He doesn't change, nor does He encourage us to change.

> "For I am the LORD, I do not change."
>
> — MALACHI 3:6

> "Jesus Christ is the same yesterday, today, and forever."
>
> — HEBREW 13:8

To the contrary, God always calls His people to *return* — to go back and rediscover the ancient paths that lead to God and to His Word.

> "Remember these, O Jacob, and Israel, for you are My servant; I have formed you, you are My servant; O Israel, you will not be forgotten by Me! I have blotted out, like a thick cloud, your transgressions, and like a cloud, your sins. Return to Me, for I have redeemed you."
>
> — ISAIAH 44:21-22

> "Go and proclaim these words toward the north, and say: 'Return, backsliding Israel,' says the LORD; 'I will not cause My anger to fall on you. For I am merciful,' says the LORD; I will not remain angry forever."
>
> — JEREMIAH 3:12

When His people come to realize their error and need for Him, they don't say, "Let's change." They say, "Come let us **return** unto the LORD and He will heal us" (Hos. 6:1).

But on the night of his election to the presidency, Obama said, "Change has come to America." We wholeheartedly agree that in fact, it has. True to his word, Obama and his administration set out to "fundamentally transform America," which suggests they set out to transform—change—the fundamentals of America; specifically, the foundational principles upon which the nation was built and sustained. Change has indeed come to America, but what kind and to what end? What does "change" look like in the end? Compared to restoration, it would hint that the intentions of Progressives and like-minded people are not necessarily faithful to the constitutional principles that have guided this nation thus far.

Change, by definition, suggests that things of the past are to be replaced with something else, something new. In the current political context, and based on what has transpired legislatively in the past few years, it would seem that "change" means to do away with the America of the past and replace it with something unintended by the founders of the nation and framers of the Constitution.

In short, the pledge to "fundamentally transform America" means to abandon the covenant previously made with the Creator. This is precisely what is happening here in America. We now find that, as a nation, we are changing our focus and going after other "gods." We are turning away from the one and only God, and, consequently, reenacting the egregious error committed by Israel so long ago.

AMERICA'S GREAT CRISIS

In spite of what politicians and pundits would have us believe, America is in the midst of a major, multi-faceted crisis. It is moral, domestic, international, financial, agricultural and spiritual in nature, manifesting in so many ways that it is hard to keep up with it all. But just to name a few, we are seeing corrupt and inept leadership (in both parties), natural disasters, and a general dissolution of societal norms. This is what happens when a righteous nation begins to go after other gods or allows other gods to be viewed as acceptable, even preferred over the one true God.

When all religions are considered equal; when all relationships, whether biblical or not, are considered equal; when certain species of fish are protected by law, but unborn babies are not, it is indicative of a nation that has changed; a nation that has turned from the Tree of Life and is desiring the "wisdom" of the fruit of the Tree of Knowledge of Good and Evil. However, as Scripture warns:

"There is a way which seems right to a man, but its end is the way of death."

– Proverbs 14:12

No one intentionally sets out to embrace death. That would be overtly foolish. However, because the Adversary is good at what he does, appealing to man with that which appears to be good, and because man's heart is "wicked from his youth," death is what men typically run toward thinking they are embracing life. It could be put this way:

"For my people are foolish, they have not known me; they are silly children, and they have no understanding. They are wise to do evil, but to do good they have no knowledge."

– Jeremiah 4:22

When the people forget who they are and where they came from, or more importantly, when they forget who and what sustained them and brought them to where they are, they will disregard the reality of the past, question and challenge accepted moral values, and reject any standard that will not accommodate their passions and desires. They want "change" that permits them to do what they wish to do, even if that requires redefining what marriage is or challenging the notion that an unborn child is actually a child. When that happens, you may be sure that we have arrived at the day which Isaiah described when God warned those in His vineyard to beware:

"Woe to those who call evil good, and good evil; who put darkness for light, and light for darkness; who put bitter for sweet, and sweet for bitter! Woe to those who are wise in their own eyes, and prudent in their own sight! … Who justify the wicked for a bribe, and take away justice from the righteous man! Therefore as the fire devours the stubble, and the flame consumes the chaff, so their root will be as rottenness, and their blossom will ascend like dust: because they have rejected the law of the LORD of hosts, and despised the word of the Holy One of Israel."

– Isaiah 5:20-21, 23-24

Imagine going from being His chosen vineyard to being a people who reward evil thought and deed and disdain and excoriate good. Of course, their love for evil must be concealed with the veneer of "good." Anything less would be overt, and the Adversary doesn't work that way—"The serpent was the most subtle of all the beasts of the field" (Gen.3:1). So living in a culture that cries for and even demands tolerance and co-existence—things presented as "good"—we as believers need to remember that the tare is not sown among the wheat so that the wheat and tare may co-exist in harmony and tolerance. That is merely the ploy which allows the tare to take root and fulfill its purpose—"to steal, kill and destroy." To ignore this reality in America hastens our demise. We only have to look to Great Britain to see our future if we continue on this path.

Great Britain used to be a strong, Christian nation that believed in the rule of law and the sovereignty of God's Word. America, in fact, inherited her love and reverence for freedom, liberty and the rule of law from our British cousins. But today's Britain is quite different. Decades ago the decision was made to allow and tolerate other faiths, ideologies and customs even while younger Britons were losing faith in God and the Bible.

In conjunction with this decline of Christianity and the love for tolerance came the Islamic invasion. The result: empty and dying churches were sold to Muslims and became mosques. Now, decades later, Muslims boldly march in the streets promoting Islam, jihad and other Islamic doctrines while Christians are bound by law to keep relatively silent under the threat of prosecution by the British government. The tares do what they are designed to do—"steal, kill and destroy."

This, unfortunately, is where America is headed as we so boldly turn away from the God of Israel. Consider what has transpired in the last fifty years where atheists are concerned. First, it was removing prayer from schools; now it is pastors being threatened with legal suits because of what they say in their own pulpits. Are the atheists in America content with the concessions that have been made to them through the decades, or do they want to assert more influence and gain more power over people of faith?

Is the homosexual community content with the concessions that have been granted to them over the decades, or do they desire even more concessions? You should see the point. These groups will NEVER be satisfied until they have silenced God's people and eradicated the established moral boundaries set in place by our founders and inspired by God's Word. Folks, this is what change looks like!

According to a recent news report, corroborated by a video uploaded to YouTube, a young lesbian actress confronted a street preacher in New York, and while shouting expletives, made the comment, "The Tea Party, ultra-creepy Christians and conservatives—you are the reason America is in trouble." While ultimate responsibility for the nation's ills does fall on God's people (2 Chron. 7:14), the point is that her diatribe against the preacher reveals the nature and intent of the heart of those who want change. The people who hold to more traditional/biblical views are considered to be the problem standing in the way of the America they wish to bring about. "If those people who look to the past were out of the way, we'd have the change that we want."

That corrupt mindset is typical of a growing breed of Americans and indicates that we are a nation in flux. Like a man in the midst of a mid-life crisis who goes so far as to buy the proverbial red sports car and leave the wife of his youth, America has abandoned what is faithful, true and steadfast in favor of something—anything—that satiates her carnal passions.

We have and are being promised "change." We are challenged to go "Forward." In fact, that was the motto for the Democratic Party in the 2012 election cycle! We are made to feel a little embarrassed if we look up to or speak honorably of our founders and forefathers. Today they are called a bunch of old, rich, dead, white men who were bigots and sexists. Subtly, we are being seduced to forget and disregard the foundation in exchange for something that makes us "feel good."

Sadly, today's America is tired of the old ways and traditions. She wants something new, younger and hip. When it comes to the belief in American Exceptionalism, progressive thinkers consider that to be ignorant, patriotic rhetoric and an embarrassment to an enlightened mindset. In fact, they feel we should be apologizing to all the other nations for being American. You might say there are quite a number of Americans who don't wish to be identified as such but would prefer to be like all the other nations of Europe and abroad. This is what "change" looks like.

THE EYES OF ALL PEOPLE ARE UPON US

It is clear that, by and large, as a nation we have turned away from God and have forsaken Him. What everyone should be fearfully pondering is whether He has turned away from us. Has He forsaken America? If so, what does this mean for the future of the Republic? This thought brings to mind what Winthrop wrote on the deck of the *Arbella*:

> We must consider that we shall be as a City upon a Hill, the eyes of all people are upon us; so that if we shall deal falsely with our God in this work we have undertaken and so cause Him to withdraw His present help from us, we shall be made a story and a by-word through the world."

According to Messiah, a city upon a hill "cannot be hidden." It is there for all to see, friend and foe alike. If America is that "city upon a hill" and the eyes of the world are upon us, what are they supposed to see? From God's point of view, the world should be able to observe and desire the benefits bestowed upon a nation who serves God faithfully—prosperity, peace and power. This is exactly the purpose Moses alluded to in the wilderness when he told Israel:

> "Surely I have taught you statutes and judgments, just as the Lord my God commanded me that you should act according to them in the land which you go to possess. Therefore be careful to observe them; for this is your wisdom and your understanding in the sight of the peoples who will hear all these statutes, and say, 'Surely this great nation is a wise and understanding people.' For what great nation is there that has God so near to it, as the Lord our God is to us, for whatever reason we may call upon Him?

> And what great nation is there that has such statutes and righteous judgments as are in all this law which I set before you this day? Only take heed to yourself, and diligently keep yourself, lest you forget the things your eyes have seen, and lest they depart from your heart all the days of your life. And teach them to your children and your grandchildren."
>
> – Deuteronomy 4:5-9

Moses' message seems to be this: all the things you have learned in the past are the very things that will sustain you in the future. Be true to them and you will reap the benefits of life, liberty and the pursuit of happiness. Not only that, but others around you — the nations — will be inspired to know the God of Israel because of your obedience and reward. They will be watching you.

This, ladies and gentlemen, was also Winthrop's message. This is what he was warning his fellow Puritans about. He was not commending them for being favored of God. He was alerting them of the responsibility that goes with God's favor and the repercussions of failure to be true to it.

So, what happens to the favored nation that fails to honor Him who bestowed the favor? What becomes of the nation that indulges in every vice and form of wickedness to His dishonor — and for all to see? Winthrop said they would become a story and "byword," a phrase Moses used to warn Israel of the consequence of breaking covenant with God:

> "And you shall become an astonishment, a proverb, and a byword among all the nations where the LORD will drive you."
>
> – Deuteronomy 28:37

If Israel turned from God, they would be mocked and ridiculed by the nations. They would be taunted and jibed, and no one would respect them. Ironically, their desire to be like everyone else and to be liked by everyone else would result in their being despised by everyone else. They made the false assumption that they could do what was right in their own eyes and all would be well. To the contrary, the result was rejection and death. That outcome seems similar to one where a person who is warned not to eat the fruit of a forbidden tree chooses to believe that "it is good for food, pleasant to the eye and desirable to make one wise." Eve and her husband learned all too late that what seems right to man often results in death.

On that note, it wasn't the serpent in the garden that separated Adam and Eve from God. He merely appealed to a hidden desire. True, he spun the lie and seduced the woman, but she determined that the tree was desirable. Adam made the decision to eat the deadly fruit even though he knew the probable outcome. The point is, though Satan wanted to destroy them, he didn't have the authority to do it. Instead he successfully created a situation whereby they destroyed themselves. In the end it wasn't an external force that brought about their demise. It was their own internal passion that led them to turn from God.

In a similar vein, Balaam couldn't curse Israel because God had blessed them; but he could devise a plan whereby they would bring a curse upon themselves at Baal Peor. Balaam's wicked heart is revealed by the fact that he counseled Balak to send the beautiful daughters of Moab and Midian into the camp of Israel. Yet, the plague that ensued was unleashed because many of God's people were led astray by the beauty of the foreign women and the lure of their gods (Num 25:1-3).

As in the garden, this demonstrates that God's covenant people can't be cursed by others because they don't have that kind of authority over God's people. However, others do have the power to seduce His people away from the truth, with the end result being that His people bring a curse and death upon themselves.

Might it be this way for America? If God has blessed America, and if we have been in covenant with Him, can others curse her and render her doom, or shall wayward and changing America bring the curse upon her own head? In 1837, Abraham Lincoln forewarned:

> "At what point then is the approach of danger to be expected? I answer, if it ever reach us, it must spring up amongst us; it cannot come from abroad. If destruction be our lot we must ourselves be its author and finisher. As a nation of freemen we must live together through all time, or die by suicide."

THE UNCIVIL WAR

To be fair, it should be noted that change has been part of the American experience for quite some time. In fact, the root cause of the change we see today has been slowly percolating beneath the surface since the founding of the republic. Though it may come as a surprise to some, there have long been two diametrically opposed ideologies existing within our borders and houses of government. Some consider it diversity. Some call it a consequence of being a melting pot, but for our purposes we'll call it the "two opposite Americas." You can find elements of these two Americas in the very beginning of our development by simply comparing Jamestown with Plymouth.

Of the 144 men who first settled Jamestown, only one was a minister, Robert Hunt, and he died within the first year. Frankly, in spite of all the profession for advancing the Christian faith in its charter, the Virginia Company's main purpose for launching this venture was to establish a settlement that would grow tobacco and render a profit. Most of those who came to Jamestown had that same objective.

In some instances, when they should have been learning the land and how to grow food to sustain them, they were off looking for riches. This is why, in large part, they were forced to kidnap natives and hold them for ransom—that is, food—to get them through the winter. In short, Jamestown was about "stuff" more than anything else and may be why today there is no Jamestown, Virginia. Only a historical park and archaeological site exists where Jamestown once was.

On the other hand, there is a municipality called Plymouth, Massachusetts, and that is likely due to the fact that those who settled this community came looking not for stuff, but for substance. They came intending to plant a community of faith and covenantal relationship with God and one another. Like Jamestown, they suffered through difficult times, but unlike Jamestown, they survived and eventually thrived.

So in this comparison we see that from our beginning there have been two Americas—two views of life diametrically opposed to one another. One leads to life and the other to death. The same is true today, though we see these two opposite views manifested in somewhat different ways. We also find that, in some cases, both "opposites" grow on the same Tree of the Knowledge of Good and Evil, just on opposite sides; for example, Democrats & Republicans or Liberals & Conservatives. Of course, there is also the issue of ethnicity and race, which can determine what category above one chooses to align themselves with.

The point of this is to show that eventually the opposition of one of these groups to the other leads to conflict. When a nation no longer views itself as "one nation under God," but a nation of groups, subgroups and factions all desiring change, conflict is bound to erupt and life will get ugly.

Consider the global scene: there is and has always been a huge disconnect between those in the East and those in the West. Many of us remember the days of the Iron Curtain over Europe and the Cold War between the West and the Soviet Union. Unfortunately, this disconnect, division and opposition is a reality of life. But when we see ourselves as one people in God because we are in covenant with Him and one another, this division and strife doesn't have to continue. This sentiment brings to mind a poem by Rudyard Kipling that seems rather apropos.

> "Oh, East is East, and West is West, and never the twain shall meet, 'Till Earth and Sky stand presently at God's great Judgment Seat; But there is neither East nor West, Border, nor Breed, nor Birth, When two strong men stand face to face, tho' they come from the ends of the earth!"

Unfortunately, man's heart is wicked from his youth, and seldom does a majority of people come to realize the need for coming together as one under the One True God. That is what makes the story of America so unique. Men came together in the face of hardship and struggle and ignited a noble effort to become one people. Men and women from different nations and various backgrounds, striving to be one people, united under one law, serving One God, is why *E Pluribus Unum*—"Out of many, one"—was written upon the Great Seal of the United States.

In 1861, that concept was tested to the breaking point. The Union dissolved, and the country was embroiled in a great Civil War because as Abraham Lincoln saw it:

> "We have forgotten God. We have forgotten the gracious Hand which preserved us in peace, and multiplied and enriched and strengthened us; and we have vainly imagined, in the deceitfulness of our own hearts, that all these blessings were produced by some superior wisdom and virtue of our own....It behooves us then to humble ourselves before the offended Power, to confess our national sins and to pray for clemency and forgiveness."

Oddly enough, the American Civil War is another of those strange parallels between America and Israel. After Solomon died, his son, Rehoboam, came to power. Following the counsel of his younger advisers, he informed the nation of Israel that the burdens they had endured under Solomon would be multiplied under his reign. In other words, he intended to rule them ruthlessly as their master, with them being his servants. This resulted in a rebellion and subsequent split in the nation. Ten tribes formed the northern kingdom of Israel under Jeroboam, leaving Rehoboam to reign over the southern kingdom of Judah (1 Kings 12:1-24).

In an even more fascinating parallel, David and Solomon each reigned over Israel for forty years, which means that eighty years after David began to rule, the kingdom of Israel divided into north and south. For all practical purposes, the American Revolution ended in the fall of 1781 with the defeat of the British under Lord Cornwallis at Yorktown, Virginia. Eighty years later in 1861, Confederate artillery batteries fired on Union forces stationed at Fort Sumter, South Carolina, igniting the Civil War. Just as ancient Israel's division became a contest between North and South, so too was America's greatest trial, a division that continued—some would argue, has continued—for many decades.

Today the nation is divided again, which is evidenced by the constant clamor for "change." There is a distinction, though, between the division we see now as opposed to the Civil War era. This time the boundary is not determined by the Mason-Dixon Line. For some time now, it has been determined by economic, racial, religious, political and social issues.

Most people remember that in the wake of the 2000 presidential election debacle, the nation was literally divided into two camps. Though distinct in nature, the division was oddly reminiscent of the fallout the nation experienced after the 1860 general election and the ascendency of Abraham Lincoln.

In 1860 it was "North and South." In 2000 it was more "Republican and Democrat." As a result of the 2000 election, the US Senate was equally divided 50/50, very much resembling the nation in 1860. Both Abraham Lincoln and George W. Bush reluctantly became war-time presidents, both being hailed and hated by many. In 2000 and beyond, Bush was lampooned by his detractors as a buffoon and considered to be "unintelligent" and "ignorant" by his political enemies. Actually, compared to the names and epithets railed at Lincoln, that was pretty tame.

The point is, both men were castigated and verbally abused by their enemies without restraint, and the nation was bitterly divided along political lines. In 1861, that political division erupted into bloodshed. In 2001, many wondered how long it would be before the division and strife repeated the violence of the 1860 pattern. It was suggested then that if violence were to erupt, "the distinction will be that battle lines will not be determined by geographical boundaries but by ideology. Your mortal enemy won't necessarily be in another region of the country but may be right next door or even in your own home."

With many years having passed since those days, the internal division and social chasms have only grown deeper and more intense. Perhaps not since the Civil War has there been such division and potential for bloodshed among neighbors as what we currently see in our nation. We may not see widespread violence and bloodshed on the fields of Manassas, Shiloh and Gettysburg, but every day the threat of conflict exists within our schools, courthouses and city streets across the country.

Might it be because "change" has encouraged us to tell the Prince of Peace He is not welcome in our schools, courthouses and public squares? This point, in a nutshell, explains why there is such deep division and disunity in America. We can only be one if we are under One God. That's the way a covenant functions and why "change" is so detrimental to our national health.

A husband, wife and their family cannot live in harmony if one of the parties has decided to embrace another lover or two. Covenant requires exclusivity and nothing less. To flirt with other relationships is to bring division, conflict, and if unrepentant, destruction. Likewise, because there are people in America who have decided to come out from under His sovereignty and turn to other "lovers," they have sown division and strife in the nation. By turning to other philosophies and beliefs, they must, by default, be at war with Him and His people.

Shall we put it this way? There are tares sown in the wheat, and they are not sown in order to co-exist in peace and harmony with the wheat—they are there to steal, kill and destroy. In that vein, allow us to share a few more examples of what "change" looks like through specific events over the last few years that expose America's wayward mindset, our on-going moral collapse and the incendiary disposition of our once-great nation.

WHEN GOOD IS EVIL AND EVIL IS GOOD

In our culture, advocacy groups are a dime a dozen. People are always championing the rights of something or someone whom they believe to be downtrodden and oppressed. Yet, have you noticed how very few of these groups defend biblical principles? Have you noticed just how hypocritical most of them really are? Take PETA for instance. This group (People for the Ethical Treatment of Animals) is extremely aggressive in its war to defend the rights of animals. They wage relentless campaigns against hunters, meat-eaters and furriers, yet they take no official position on the slaughter of unborn babies. Their position is to have no position on the issue.

Even so, PETA is viewed by many, and especially by the Hollywood elites, as "good." At the same time, these elitists consider a person who protests against abortion as a right-wing religious fanatic—"evil." As you know, this way of thinking is not exceptional but is fast becoming the accepted norm.

In September 2011, a Fort Worth, Texas high school student was sent to the principal's office and spent a day in in-school suspension for telling another classmate he believes homosexuality is wrong. According to the student, "We were talking about religions. I said, 'I'm a Christian. I think being a homosexual is wrong,' " He said his statement was spoken to a friend sitting behind him. Unfortunately for the student, his teacher overheard him, started yelling at him and sent him to the office where, apparently, those in charge thought he should be suspended.

This kind of reaction to a student who holds to "traditional values" isn't an isolated incident. It is now the standard in society. So in today's world, an honor student who holds to the biblical view of homosexuality is considered evil. He is construed as a bigot and guilty of "hate speech," while those who wholeheartedly embrace the gay agenda are considered virtuous and good.

In San Francisco, a city where being gay is widely celebrated, public nudity is becoming chic. In the city by the bay, this practice is not only lawful but is staunchly defended. At the same time, circumcision, a biblically endorsed practice for those in covenant with God, is frowned upon and disparaged by the city fathers. In fact, the San Francisco city council tried to outlaw circumcision even as they defended the right of its citizens to parade around in the buff displaying their...um... uncircumcision. Again, "good is evil and evil is good."

Since we are speaking of California, a few years ago an Orange County, California family was fined $300 for holding Bible studies at their home because it violated a city zoning code. According to San Juan Capistrano city officials, a special permit must be obtained in order to host such events IN THEIR OWN HOME! How absolutely ridiculous it has become when government is permitted to essentially outlaw Bible studies, first in public schools and now in private homes. Still, this is the nature of the spiritual war Americans—certainly believers in America—find themselves in. This is what "change" looks like! Government is not the only culprit seeking to curtail, or at least discourage, the worship of the God of Abraham, Isaac and Jacob. Now, certain elements of the religious establishment are also participating in the assault on "traditional values" and faith. A recent example is an event that was billed as an interfaith prayer vigil held at Washington's National Cathedral in commemoration of the 10th anniversary of the September 11 attacks. This service included the Bishop of Washington, a rabbi, an incarnate lama, a Buddhist nun, a Hindu priest, the president of the Islamic Society of North America, a Muslim musician and an Imam; but not one evangelical Christian was invited.

A spokesperson for the Cathedral admitted that evangelicals were purposely omitted from the program stating that "diversity was first and foremost" a factor in the planning, and the event would be a "secular service." We need to point out here that by "diversity" they meant to tolerate everyone's opinion, theologies and philosophies. In Bible-speak this is equivalent to "mixing" the holy with the profane or, as Paul puts it, being "unequally yoked." Yet, this seems to be the trend in certain pockets of Christianity. No wonder, considering how the first openly gay Presbyterian minister interprets Scripture:

> "There's no longer a right viewpoint and a wrong viewpoint but several faithful viewpoints, one of which includes me in terms of being a minister in the Presbyterian Church. So we're honoring a diversity of viewpoints in our church."

In other words, tolerance and diversity supersede sound doctrine, at least as far as some are concerned. Nevertheless, we are to understand that though culture may call it "good," the Creator calls this "evil," even if it defies the clergy claiming to represent Him. No wonder there is such division, strife and confusion when such "ministers" speak in concert with those who have contempt for sound biblical doctrine.

There are many other similar stories and incidents that we could relate to you, but here is the point: America has strayed so far from the moral principles that helped guide the Founders that, short of miraculous and divine interposition, the country we once knew and loved will collapse into chaos and madness and, dare we say, civil war.

LEFT IS LEFT; RIGHT IS RIGHT, AND NEVER THE TWAIN SHALL MEET

When the so-called Tea Party was rallying against the Affordable Care Act (a.k.a. Obamacare) and the Democratic legislative agenda, their ranks were accused of anything and everything as they were jeered by the left as "thugs" and by Rep. Nancy Pelosi as "Nazis" (her district includes the city of San Francisco). She even claimed that Tea Party people threatened and spat upon Democratic members of Congress as they prepared to vote on the Health Care bill. Not long after, another California Democratic Representative, Maxine Waters, said the Tea Party should be consigned to the infernal regions (though those were not her exact words).

Also, Teamster's President, Jimmy Hoffa, told a crowd of Obama supporters that unions, workers and the left were in **a war** with the right-wing. Hoffa said, "President Obama, this is your army. We are ready to march. . . . Let's take these (expletive referring to tea party candidates) out!" One might assume that this kind of language was hyperbole, but then again, maybe not. It is certain that we are in the throes of a spiritual conflict. Consequently, in the physical realm, it would seem that civility, common courtesy and agreeing to disagree are things of the past. We are in the midst of an uncivil war and should be alerted to the determination and tactics of our opponents.

In February 2011, tens of thousands of people converged on the state capital of Wisconsin to protest legislation that was aimed at fixing the state's budget woes. Included in the proposed bill were limitations on the collective bargaining rights of state employees, i.e. unions. This caused as many as 100,000 people to literally occupy the Capitol building and set up sleeping quarters, food stations and an information center. The protesters were loud, rude, aggressive and destructive. It was reported that clean up and repairs to the Capitol cost upwards of eight million dollars. In some cases, the protesters—or at least a few of them—became threatening. One woman was arrested for sending death threats to Republican lawmakers, and .22 caliber ammunition was found in the Capitol and other state buildings.

Throughout the demonstrations, the protesters continually chanted, "This is what democracy looks like," and even likened their protests to that of the Egyptian dissidents who marched for the overthrow of Hosni Mubarek. In Wisconsin, we saw how very close the nation came to violence when "liberal" and "conservative" ideology clashed. According to some of the protesters, occupation and destruction of state property and threats of violence against those who disagree with you are what "democracy looks like"—it is most definitely what "change" looks like. So what should we expect when the division isn't political but is simply between right and wrong, good and evil? What happens to a nation when the prevailing mindset considers evil as good and good as evil? How intense will the conflict become?

THE 99%

In the same year that protesters marched on Wisconsin's Capitol, protests in New York City began, orchestrated by the so-called "Occupy Wall Street" movement. According to the "official" website, this demonstration was a "leaderless resistance movement with people of many colors, genders and political persuasions. . . . We are the 99% that will no longer tolerate the greed and corruption of the 1%. We are using the revolutionary Arab Spring tactic to achieve our ends."

Statements like these are quite bothersome and demand to be noticed even if the Occupy movement seems to have dissipated. Just because they're not in the current news cycle doesn't mean the ideology or the determination for change has dissipated. When people invoke terms like "resistance," "revolutionary," and "Arab Spring," that should cause us to be very aware of what is transpiring within our borders. We would suggest it is an indication that the tares are beginning to put forth their fruit.

According to their statements, the "resistance" was intended to inspire a revolution against the wealthy banking system and corporations. Observers reported that this revolution was calling, not for reform, but an "end to capitalism." It is important to note that while they were making these claims and voicing their objectives, they had the backing of many leftist personalities and the moral support of the highest offices in the land. No, these people and their philosophy have not gone away. They have just taken on a different persona and shape and will, eventually, pop up again with the same agenda. Understanding that, what lengths will they go to accomplish their goal if they truly intend to start a revolution? Are we talking armed struggle and civil war?

There was, in fact, a degree of violence associated with these protests in New York, in Boston and in other American cities to which this movement managed to spread, resulting in hundreds of arrests. Reports of rallies for convicted terrorists, severed "heads" on pikes, signs encouraging the killing of parents and even calls for corporate CEOs to be eaten—yes, eaten—emerged from the mayhem. It was also reported that public sex acts, wide spread drug use and extremely unsanitary conditions accompanied these protests. One address given to the crowd was delivered by a man identified as Muhammed who was said to be a "veteran" of the Egyptian uprising of that year. In this address he called for revolution and the end of capitalism, which absolutely thrilled those assembled.

So, understand that there are people in America—more than we would like to admit—who apparently identify and even sympathize with what has been going on over the last few years in the Middle East. If these revolutionaries were to embrace the tactics of the so-called "Arab Spring," would that also include beating and murdering their opponent and raping innocent bystanders as their Egyptian "brothers" did? That is exactly what happened in Egypt in 2011, and it is what is ongoing now in Iraq and Syria with the advent of ISIS.

The point here is very simple—"change" in today's political and social context means transformation, reshaping and revolution, and in a revolution, people, usually the innocent, die. During the French Revolution—which actually demonstrated what a democracy *does* look like—scores of people died. Many of them were marched to the guillotine. Most of those were the wealthy aristocracy.

What is most disturbing, yet not surprising, is that the demonstrations in America garnered the support of many Democratic leaders, including Nancy Pelosi, several Hollywood personalities (one who called for the guillotine to be utilized for bankers who make over 100 million), and worker's unions. Some reports suggest that several leftist groups actually bankrolled this effort and were the brains behind it.

However deep the involvement was, those individuals and groups who supported this in any fashion, supported the idea of a revolution that desires to end capitalism and the free-market system. This revolution desires to redistribute the wealth of these "evil corporations" and invest all power in the **workers** of America.

This proposed revolution sounds very much like another revolution of the last century initiated by men like Lenin, Trotsky, et al. In that October Revolution, which actually began in February, thousands of people died, namely the Bolshevik's political opponents, and all within the context of class warfare — looking out for the 99%. This is nothing new, actually. The idea that "they" have something "you, the oppressed," should have is as old as time itself, because that is precisely how the serpent beguiled Eve:

> "God knows that if you eat this fruit, you will be like Him, knowing good from evil."

In short, "God has something that you *should* have, but He is keeping it from you. Just ignore what He said, and take it!" It occurs to us that his tactics are alive and well today and are infecting the minds and hearts of many Americans. We would like to point out that the fall of Man may never have happened if Eve had kept her eye on the Tree of Life—but she didn't; she turned her face away from it and gazed upon the Tree of Good and Evil. As noted earlier, that decision ended up very badly for her and for Adam.

Ironically, during this "occupation," many of these protesters invoked the names of the Founders and spoke as if they were doing what the forefathers of this nation would have done in response to tyranny. In other words, these protests attempted to present themselves as good and virtuous defenders of liberty, while all the time embracing all manner of debauchery, anarchy and totalitarian views. We shouldn't be surprised though—the tare always tries to pass itself off as wheat.

When all was said and done, what were all these protests about?

What are PETA, the ACLU, the Teamsters and the atheists really advocating? It seems obvious they want what millions of Americans, including politicians, priests and paupers want—"change." Well, "change" has come and is steadily eroding the country's foundational principles. To be fair, it didn't start with the Obama administration. It started before any of us were ever born. Still, most would probably agree that since the inauguration of the Obama administration in 2009, "change" has been occurring at an accelerated and alarming rate.

So one has to wonder if the transformation we are currently undergoing is the type of "change" that those 69 million people who voted for Obama had envisioned. Based on how many are reacting to some of the policies and initiatives coming out of the White House and the halls of Congress, it would seem some are having second thoughts. Unfortunately, it is too little too late. They wanted change, and now we have it; perhaps, these changes are not conducive to the survival of the republic.

As a matter of fact, the so-called stimulus package, health care overhaul, immigration reform, and Cap & Trade initiatives were just the beginning of a long laundry list of policies intended to solidify in America a purely democratic, perhaps socialist, or in a worse-case scenario, totalitarian society. If that is so, it would spell the end of America as we have known it. It may not be what we had in mind, but it is what we have. The Adversary always dangles the "good" part of the fruit, never revealing the inherent evil within it until it's too late.

The situation is reminiscent of when the children of Israel began to despise the manna God gave them and longed for the food that Egypt had once provided them, ignoring, of course, that the same Egypt had made them all slaves. Nevertheless, their cry for a change in their diet was so great that God gave them what they wanted—until it was coming out their nostrils and they could stand it no longer. Not only that, but because they had given into their temporal cravings, effectively a renouncement of what God had provided, a plague swept through the camp killing thousands (Num.11:4-33).

That is the predictable outcome each time God's people turn away from the Tree He gave them to eat from in order to partake of the other tree. Still, it seems that God will, at times, give people what they want in order that they might see it was not what they needed. Unfortunately, for many Israelites, that revelation came too late, and it may prove to be the same for many Americans.

This story also casts a light on another component of our present circumstance. In fact, it demonstrates the primary issue that plagues us as a people and which has resulted in many of the changes we see underway. The children of Israel embraced the attitudes of a presumed minority of people referred to as a "mixed multitude."

It was these people who first began to lust after the amenities of Egypt, and before long, a large number of Israelites were infected with their poisonous mindset. The narrative in Numbers 11, as well as Exodus 16, makes it clear that the preference of many was slavery with gratification rather than freedom with contentment. In other words, they were willing to surrender their liberty to a totalitarian government who would feed them what they wanted rather than live free under a God who, acting in their best interest, would give them what they needed.

This attitude brings to mind a quote attributed to George Washington, taken from an unread portion of his inaugural speech of 1789. Washington wrote:

"America would endure until the people of America shall have lost all virtue; until they shall have become totally insensible to the difference between freedom and slavery; until they shall have been reduced to such poverty of spirit as to be willing to sell that pre-eminent blessing, the birthright of a freeman, for a mess of pottage. In short, until they have been found incapable of governing themselves and ripe for a master."

Here is what William Penn, another founding father, said:

"Those who will not be governed by God will be ruled by tyrants."

Could it be that the time Washington and Penn warned of has come? Has our arrogant disregard for His Word and His principles brought us to the brink of collapse? In our attempt to redefine laws, have we broken our covenant with Him? Please know that in presenting these examples of political and social conflict, we do not have a political ax to grind. Still, we do wish to accentuate the point that politics and social issues are a reflection of the spiritual condition of the nation.

Consider that, during the Civil War, the bitter feelings between North and South thrust the nation into armed conflict, in turn forcing the President—ironically a politician from Illinois—to trounce on certain aspects of the Constitution in order to quell the rebellion. Therefore, our hope and trust is not invested in any political party or personality but in the King of kings and Lord of lords.

That being understood, we need to still make clear that the hostile environment now present in America is what those who have other plans for America have seized upon. That these would-be kings, princes and tsars are growing in influence and power is indication that there is a serious spiritual malady affecting America—one that comes as a result of God's people turning to other gods and He, in turn, hiding His face from them. When He does that, when He removes His Presence, another presence comes in to rule in His stead.

CHAPTER SEVEN

Legal Tyranny & Lawless Laws

*"There is scarcely a king (or would-be-king) in a hundred
who would not, if he could, follow the example of Pharaoh
– get first all the people's money, then all their lands, and
then make them and all their children slaves forever."*

— THOMAS JEFFERSON

A S WE POINTED out, there have always been two Americas—two philosophies, two ideals. One we would align with
the heart and soul evident in the lives of men like Bradford
and Winthrop. The other would be evidenced by those in Jamestown
who, though lovers of freedom's benefits, did not commit themselves
wholly to freedom's responsibilities.

Throughout America's history, there have been those from the latter
camp and mindset that, because they want the blessings of the covenant—desiring to own the vineyard for themselves without paying
the price for it—have proposed radical means of seizing ownership
and control; namely, "let's kill the heir!"

At times, this radical element have reared their heads only to be
quickly put down by the more traditional forces in the country, thus
preserving some semblance of what the Founders had hoped American
society would be. Nevertheless, in the last part of the 20th century,
and certainly within the last decade, we have witnessed how even
those considered to be on the conservative side of the political aisle

have done their fair share in undermining the principles upon which the nation was established, as well.

For example, it is becoming apparent that the vast majority of Americans, regardless of race, cultural background or political affiliation, have succumbed to the myth that the Founders established a democracy—a society where the citizens can arbitrarily make or change law when it best suits the will of the majority. This is not just parsing words. It is a critical shift in our mindset and one that betrays the fact that we are abandoning the principles of covenant with God and one another.

DEMOCRACY OR REPUBLIC?

To underscore the severity of the situation our nation is facing, it is important for the reader to understand that the Founding Fathers did **not** establish a democracy but a republic. That we might emphasize the importance as it relates to our subject, let us briefly distinguish the differences between the two philosophies.

First, you should know that in using the terms *democratic* or *republican*, we are **not** speaking of political parties but philosophies. In today's world, even Republican Party leaders nefariously refer to our system of government as a democracy as if that is what it was always intended to be. Therefore, the objective here is not to advance or denigrate any political party but to demonstrate what was intended by the founders and, consequently, expose the purpose and potential dangers of "change" as it is being manifested today.

The word *democracy* means "people rule." On the surface that may sound lofty, idealistic and noble, but the reality is that there is an explicit danger in true democracy. In both a direct and representative style of democracy, the majority's power is absolute and unlimited, which means that law is fluid. Depending on the will of the electorate or the elective, laws can ebb and flow like water as it is moved upon by the shifting winds of public opinion.

It also means that the minority would be considered to be of no consequence and would find themselves in the undesirable position of having to conform to the majority's will in order to survive. In extreme circumstances, the minority who holds fast to their dissenting position might find themselves being castigated and labeled as society's unco-operative and undesirable element. At that point, who can say what measures the unrestrained majority may turn to?

So then, for a purely democratic society to render justice for all, it would require that the overwhelming majority of the populace be just and moral. For if the people are noble, then presumably, their representatives and the laws they adopt will be too. Ideally, these laws would protect not only the rights of the majority but the individual as well, and for the greater good of all society. The obvious flaw in this style of government is that people are not instinctively noble or just but are, quite naturally, evil and self-serving. As we have already pointed out, Scripture says:

"The imagination of man's heart is evil from his youth."
— GENESIS 8:21

Seeing that wickedness comes naturally to mankind, what would happen in a democratic society if the majority of people became over-whelmingly corrupt? The representatives would naturally turn to corruption and forsake laws that espouse morality and justice for laws that provide convenience for the people's impulses and evil inclinations (e.g. Roe v. Wade). Does this not describe the cultural and political trends of our day? We would do well to remember the words of the 19th century Irish patriot and Member of Parliament, Daniel O'Connell, who said:

"Nothing is politically right which is morally wrong."

Therefore, it is accurate to assert that any brand of democracy as a form of government is fundamentally incapable of guarding against unlimited tyranny. Those who embrace and endorse democracy must understand that, sooner or later, the door to dominance by the majority will be opened and once ajar, will no doubt be difficult to shut. Furthermore, it matters little if the tyranny comes from one individual or a body of elected officials. It doesn't matter if it is a king or a collection of tsars. Tyranny is tyranny! As Jefferson wrote, multiple despots "will surely be as oppressive as one."

If one cares to search the historical record, he will find that the Founders realized the inherent danger of ruling by popular opinion. In short, they stood vehemently against the "excesses of democracy." The Father of the Constitution, James Madison, wrote:

> "Democracies have ever been spectacles of turbulence and contention; have ever been found incompatible with personal security or the rights of property; and have in general been as short in their lives as they have been violent in their death."

There are other such quotes in the annals of American history, but suffice it to say, the record is clear: the Founders NEVER intended that the United States be a democracy but a republic. The evidence for this is overwhelming. Recall the conversation Benjamin Franklin had with Mrs. Powell at the close of the Constitutional Convention in 1787: Franklin's response to her inquiry—"What kind of government do we have?"—was "a Republic, if you can keep it." What, then, is a republic, and what makes it so much more desirable as a form of government?

By definition it means literally, "a thing of the people" or "interests of the people." So, first consider that distinction. Where a democracy is a form of government where "people rule," a republican form of government is one that functions in the "interests of the people." That is to say, the objective is not necessarily in accordance with the people's whims but the people's needs. Madison expounded upon this distinction in the *Federalist Papers* and argued that the greater good of the people often required going against popular opinion, because public opinion is erratic at best.

> "There are moments in public affairs when the people, stimulated by some irregular passion, or some illicit advantage ... may call for measures which they themselves will afterwards be the most ready to lament and condemn."

If we could put it this way: though it will sustain them and is in their best interest, sometimes people get tired of manna and long for meat and all that Egypt has to offer. When their cry becomes great enough, they will end up getting the change they want (e.g. Affordable Care Act) only to find that it was not what they needed.

While a republican form of government is one where the voice of the people is most certainly represented, it is understood that those who represent them should, of necessity, be as Madison wrote, "... endowed with virtue and wisdom." The great statesman and author of Webster's Dictionary, Nathan Webster, said:

> "In selecting men for office, let principle be your guide. Regard not the particular sect or denomination of the candidate — look to his character...When a citizen gives his suffrage to a man of known immorality he abuses his trust; he sacrifices not only his own *interest* but that of his neighbor, he betrays the interest of his country."

So, why is this conversation important in regard to our topic and our national relationship with God? It is because these stated prerequisites for leadership and the concept of republic, in general, are principles and precepts that come to us directly from the Scripture.

When Moses selected seventy elders to aid in leadership, they were to be men whom he knew. That is to say, he was familiar with their character and integrity, and they were respected as virtuous leaders among the people. These seventy were to **bear** the burdens of leadership with Moses (Num. 11:17), not **impose** burdens upon the people as despots and the unprincipled would do. In this capacity, they were to be faithful servants of the God of Israel and, as such, were to serve the interests of the Israeli people as well.

We could put it this way: they were to love God and love their fellowman. This point now brings us to this question: who or what determined what was in the best interests of the people?

In the case of Israel, it was the code of morality, standards and ethics presented to Israel by God at Sinai — the Torah. Yet, even the Creator did not force His will upon the people. He invited them to enter into the covenant with Him, and they freely chose to do so. Those who did agree to the covenantal decrees pledged to be subject to the Law of God. By the way, this included Moses and all the governing elders. So in matters of controversy, it was not the will of the people, the elders or Moses that was deemed to be the final authority, but the Torah of God they had **all** agreed to live by.

The same principle exists in a republican form of government. It is the law of the land, in this case the U.S. Constitution, which guarantees freedom by establishing just and moral parameters for the citizenry and, even more conspicuously, their representatives in government. Where a democracy restricts the rights of the minority, a republican form of government is designed to restrict (not disregard) the will of the majority and to severely limit the powers of those in high office. It is designed to protect the individual's God-given rights, provided the individual does not seek liberties that exceed the boundaries established by the very law that secures his freedom.

We see, then, it is the Law or, in an American context, the Constitution that binds the populace together, anchors the society and serves to define what is in the interest of the people. The great orator Daniel Webster once said:

> "Justice, sir, is the great *interest* of man on earth. It is the ligament which holds civilized beings and civilized nations together."

When there have been those who have attempted to assert their power beyond what was allowed them by the Constitution, the checks and balances of our Republic have reeled them back in, for the most part. Thus, a republican form of government, though certainly not a perfect form of government, better understands the crucial and stabilizing role that the law plays in sustaining the intent of the Founders.

We say that because some political figures have argued over the last few years that, because the Founders were not all-knowing and were obviously imperfect men, the Constitution must also be fundamentally flawed. For the record, the constitutional delegates did, in fact, acknowledge their human frailties and deficiencies. Therefore, they wisely made provision for their inability to foresee all that the new republic may encounter by crafting procedures that allowed for the Constitution to be amended. In fact, George Washington, who presided over the convention, said:

"If to please the people, we offer what we ourselves disapprove, how can we afterward defend our work? Let us raise a standard to which the wise and honest can repair; the event is in the Hand of God."

There are three points in this quote that should be noted. First, Washington concedes that time would expose any flaws that might exist in their work and trusted that those who would be appointed to improve upon it would be "wise and honest." Obviously, they accepted that amendments would eventually come, but amendments built upon the established foundation, not abolition of the very principles that gave birth to a nation.

Secondly, he recognized that the will of the people could not always be trusted completely, so the standard must be that wise and honest men represent the interests of the people as a whole. Lastly, he acknowledged that, ultimately, God must lead and direct those in the future, just as they believed God had led and directed them to that point. In our view, that's not bad judgment for imperfect men.

So while it is indeed true that, "there is none righteous, no not one" (Rom. 3:10), one could, nevertheless, make the argument that these imperfect men fashioned a form of government that was based on perfect principles. We say this because our Constitution is based, in large part, upon the very principles, laws and statutes Moses and the nation of Israel were given at Sinai. As we have shown, the writings of many of our past leaders attest to this.

Because our form of government was based on the Torah that God gave to Israel and a belief that His Hand had guided those who birthed the nation, many other leaders have warned what would happen to the country if we abandoned those foundational principles and that fundamental belief. President John Adams wrote:

"Our Constitution was made only for a moral and religious people. It is wholly inadequate to the government of any other."

The Father of American Geography, Jedediah Morse wrote:

> "Whenever the pillars of Christianity shall be overthrown, our present republican forms of government, and all the blessings which flow from them, must fall with them."

American diplomat and politician, Daniel Webster, made this haunting declaration in 1837:

> "The hand that destroys the Constitution renders our Union asunder."

Of course, as we already noted, President Ronald Reagan said:

> "If we ever forget that we are one nation under God, then we will be a nation gone under."

There is not enough space here to quote the hundreds of sources that echo the same message these few noteworthy statements acknowledge—don't tamper with the foundation. So the purpose of this brief history lesson has been that we may better understand what those who laid the foundation intended for the country and, consequently, interpret the current changes for what they truly are. They are tampering with, if not negating outright, the wisdom and validity of the Constitution and, consequently, the inspiration and model for our American liberties—the Word of God.

Yet, that could happen in a pure democracy, because where the people rule the law can be discarded and replaced with something more suitable to the wishes of the people or the majority. If they conclude that laws written and established long ago are too antiquated to effectively deal with complex 21st century issues, then they will be driven to do away with them, because they presume the people of today would know better than those of yesterday.

Remember though, democratic principles have the tendency to open the door to tyranny, chaos, and eventually, lawlessness. So, Democracy or Republic? Which sounds closer to the path man would choose for himself, and which sounds closer to the path God would choose for man?

Have We Kept It?

"Whatever government is not a government of laws, is a despotism, let it be called what it may."

— Daniel Webster

Throughout our history, all presidents took the oath of office to "preserve, protect and defend the Constitution" while placing their hand on a Bible. But do we believe the Bible and its precepts, particularly acknowledging that it is a book of commandments and covenant, laws and blessings? Frankly, it is obvious to all who have any grasp of biblical principle and basic knowledge of this country's beginnings that we have, to put it mildly, lost our way.

Many of our citizens disdain any notion that God providentially orchestrated our conception, played any role in our progression, or has anything to do with our abundance and blessed way of life. In order to advance and legitimize their flawed point of view, this unbelieving segment of our society insists that our nation and ALL of its inhabitants should embrace and support their worldview and their agenda, which includes many lifestyles that Scripture abhors—and it grows worse, literally by the day.

Where our leaders are concerned, instead of standing for what is right in the face of evil and the growing immorality, they have decided to be the vanguard for these lawless mobs and wage war on the very morals and principles that helped to shape our nation. It's bad enough that there are those unbelievers who publicly endorse and promote these corrupt values, but now even those who claim to uphold traditional values have begun to capitulate to the demands of the atheists, the LGBT, Code Pink, and the like.

Sadly, many so-called conservative politicians and pundits have conceded that same-sex marriage is a battle whose outcome has already been decided. They argue that, because it inevitably will become a reality throughout the nation, there is no point in continuing to stand against the tide of popular opinion. For instance, recent advice given by a "staunch conservative" radio personality to those who would stand against this issue was, "Give up the fight. It's over." Consequently, emboldened by their success and waving the banner of liberty and equality, these homosexual couples and transgenders are poised to become part of the fabric of everyday American life alongside baseball, hot dogs, apple pie and Chevrolet.

Now considered legal and backed by the courts, they will receive the full support of the U.S. government and, in some cases, compensation and subsidies from you, the American taxpayer. Perhaps the worst of it is that, as we have already witnessed in cases around the country, they will—inspired by their string of victories in the courtroom—demand, not ask for, acceptance from us, regardless of our spiritual convictions. By acceptance, they mean condoning their behavior as acceptable.

In tandem with these demands, government at the federal, state and municipal levels, has made it known that any resistance from those with a dissenting view will not be tolerated. Specifically, Christian business owners who have balked at providing services for these marriages—e.g. photographers, bakers and boutique owners—have found themselves being sued in civil courts and prosecuted by their own government for civil rights violations. That doesn't even take into account the many threats of violence they receive from those who find their biblically correct positions "intolerant" and "bigoted."

THE FFRF AND THE IRS

Now consider another development. Just recently, the IRS agreed to amend its policies in regard to how it enforces tax law on churches in order to appease the demands being made by the Freedom From Religion Foundation, an atheist group that has long waged war against what they consider "rogue political churches." Basically, FFRF wants to censor what priests, pastors, rabbis and other clergy say in their sermons by threatening an IRS challenge of their tax-exempt status.

Presently, it remains unclear just what this will mean long-term, but given the fact that the IRS has proven to be antagonistic toward those with a conservative view and has agreed to adjust their standards to the satisfaction of this group, you can be sure that churches and religious organizations will most likely have to walk a tight rope when it comes to voicing political views and engaging in political activity.

The irony of this situation is that those who so vehemently insist upon enforcement of the separation of church and state (mind you, a mythical concept made viable only by a complete rewrite of history) have taken issues of morality, once considered to be the domain of the church and Scripture, and have made them the domain of the state.

In other words, though they claim to advocate a strict separation between the two, they invaded the church in order to dictate what we can preach and discuss in our congregations. This tactic, if it continues to flourish, will place a muzzle on the mouths of many of God's people in churches, ministries, synagogues and even websites, with the ultimate goal being to provoke conformity to their way of thinking.

Until now, the provisions granted to and the stipulations required of religious groups by their tax-exempt status have supported the constitutional right given to houses of worship in America to preach and promote anything short of an outright endorsement of a political candidate. But now, through the efforts of FFRF and others, even that freedom is being challenged. If the FFRF and other such groups have their way, the IRS will question and, perhaps, revoke the tax-exempt status of churches and other houses of worship if they preach on moral issues in a way that has, according to FFRF, "political implications." This is, in a word, tyranny. This is evidence of the "evil and troubles (*tzars*) that shall befall you."

We have now come to the place in history where an American pastor or rabbi may place his congregation and their place of worship in financial jeopardy if he is faithful to Scripture. If he dares to say anything from the pulpit that counters the culture's perverted mindset and their obsession with "tolerance," or more particularly, if he should resist the notion that same-sex marriage is lawful, everything that his congregation has accumulated under their tax-exempt status could be seized by the government. Furthermore, given the aggressive nature of these groups and the prevailing attitude of our leaders toward biblical standards, the clergyman would likely face civil suits and criminal charges. In this regard, it is a scary time in America and the world.

Confronting Tyranny on Lexington Green

In sharp contrast to where we are now with the attempts to silence spiritual leaders, it was the church pulpits, the men who stood in them, and the truth of God's Word proclaimed from them that shaped the moral fiber of this nation and played an integral part in its formation. In fact, the convictions and sermons of one particular pastor in Lexington, Massachusetts, played a monumental role in the events that led to the first shots of the Revolution in April, 1775.

From the passage of the Stamp Act in 1765 until that April morning skirmish on Lexington Green, the Reverend Jonas Clark had become the town's principal leader in its town meetings and issues of liberty. His home was a frequent meeting place for men like Samuel Adams (Father of the American Revolution) and John Hancock (Clark's wife's cousin and President of the Continental Congress in July, 1776). As a matter of fact, Adams and Hancock were at Reverend Clark's home on the night of April 18, 1775, when Paul Revere arrived to warn them of the approaching British regulars.

History records that, on this very night, one of Clark's house guests asked him if the Lexington people would fight if need be. Clark, who through his sermons had cultivated among his parishioners a duty to defend God-given and inalienable rights, is said to have responded, "I have trained them for this very hour!" In fact, it was his teaching of Scripture and its relationship to the issues of the day that helped his congregants recognize the difference between liberty and tyranny.

Reverend Clark's role in the conception of the American Revolution should not be underestimated and is highlighted by the fact that the first shots of the entire war were fired on his church lawn! Later, he would proclaim, "From this day (April 19) will be dated the liberty of the world!"

This history lesson should not be construed as a call to arms or as an advocacy for revolution. It is merely to point out just how far we have drifted morally as a nation and just how shrewdly and successfully the enemies of God have rewritten our national history. We have gone from being a nation that believed God's Word was to be revered and followed and that those He gave us as leaders should be respected, to a nation that disdains the very idea that the Bible is authoritative and the ultimate pattern for how we should live.

The very fact that this belligerent group, the Freedom from Religion Foundation, refers to themselves as such gives us insight to their view of Scriptural principle and law — to them it is bondage and needs to be cast off at all costs. Thus the Psalmist says:

> "The kings of the earth set themselves, and the rulers take counsel together, against the LORD, and against his anointed, saying, 'Let us break their bands asunder, and cast away their cords from us.'"

> — PSALM 2:2-3

Ironic isn't it? They are revolting against the very principles that won us liberty, granted us prosperity, and gave them the right to make such egregious accusations. It was the pulpit that helped the colonists to recognize the tyranny of King George and inspired them to declare, "We have no King but Jesus!" Now, many of their descendants wish to silence those same pulpits and force believers into compliance with their twisted mindset so that the FFRF, their supporters and confederates may be freed from what they perceive to be an unfair, bigoted, and tyrannical code of law—the Bible.

They do so, perhaps never realizing and certainly never acknowledging, that they are enforcing their own form of tyranny on us. Moreover, their arrogant disposition and ruthless methods proclaim to their enemies, though in a distorted application, the same message adopted as a rallying cry and symbol of the American Revolution— Join or Die!

So, we must ask the question: "Have we kept it?" Have we kept intact what Franklin and others worked and fought so hard to establish? Have we been faithful as a nation to uphold the standards and principles that God ordained—principles and ordinances that, when respected and obeyed, are rewarded with "life, liberty and the pursuit of happiness"? Even more importantly, have we kept the covenant our ancestors made with the God of Abraham, Isaac and Jacob?

When Lawlessness Becomes Law

"Civil tyranny is usually small at the beginning, like 'the drop of a bucket,' till at length, like a mighty torrent, or the raging waves of the sea, it bears down all before it, and deluges whole countries and empires."

– Jonathan Mayhew, Puritan minister, 1765

Though quite the understatement these days, it needs to be voiced again and again; America has entered into a very dangerous time! As the republic wanes and democracy encroaches, tyranny cannot be very far behind. To some degree, we already see it. Our leaders now rule by opinion and not by law because, as it has already been demonstrated, they pick and choose which elements of the law they wish to enforce. If it doesn't suit their agenda and opinion, they simply ignore it and refuse to uphold it. They circumvent the tenets of the Constitution or disregard it outright.

Over the last several years, presidents have begun to rule by executive order, often discounting the consensus of Congress, thus bypassing the checks and balances of our system set in place by the Founders to restrict just such an action. The wisdom of "separation of powers" was to prevent any of the three branches of government from attaining too much power.

Unfortunately, over the decades, that concept has far too often been scorned when a particular agenda is to be advanced, and most often, the power grab has come from the Executive Branch—the Presidency. Apparently, this is nothing new, because close to 200 years ago, Daniel Webster said:

"The contest, for ages, has been to rescue liberty from the grasp of executive power."

We could argue that other branches of government are just as tyrannical in their approach to governing the people. For years now, a radical judiciary has ruled by decree from the bench, often negating the will of the people, as in the revocation of California's Proposition 8, a state law prohibiting same sex marriage. In this case, the judiciary enforced their political will upon the people of California by over-riding their overwhelming support of this law.

There have been countless legal decisions handed down that ignore historical and legal precedent, not to mention allowing for the advancement of unscriptural and immoral agendas. Ironically, these radical decisions oftentimes label previous law as being "unconstitutional." It makes one wonder if, when a law contradicts their opinion, they don't just contrive a way to brand it as going against the Constitution even though their opinion is far removed from what the Founders envisioned. It seems we have arrived at the day when good is evil and evil is good; lawlessness has become the law of the land.

Thomas Jefferson was right. Tyranny does not have to be embodied in one individual. It is just as evil and just as effective when it is embodied in a group of individuals, whether the chief executives or a federal district judge—or John Q. Citizen. You see, what occurs in Washington, our state capitals and courtrooms across the country, for good or evil, is a reflection of what goes on down on Main Street, USA.

If those who govern pick and choose which of the laws they wish to enforce and those they wish to ignore, it is a reflection of the fact that God's people do the same. We are told in His word that healing of the land is predicated upon God's people—not the world—turning from their "wicked ways" (2 Chr. 7:14). Messiah warned His people of picking and choosing what to obey and what not when He said:

> "And unto the angel of the church of the Laodiceans write: These things says the Amen, the faithful and true witness, the beginning of the creation of God; I know your works, that you are neither cold nor hot: I could wish that you were cold or hot. So then because you are lukewarm, and neither cold nor hot, I will vomit you out of my mouth."
>
> – REVELATION 3:14-16

Here He is telling them they are "mixed." Laodicea's problem wasn't that they totally disregarded God and His Word. Their problem was that they mixed what God said with what someone else said. They were not totally wicked but they were not totally righteous, either.

They took the "hot" of righteousness and cooled it down with the "cold" of wickedness, inferring that they picked from God's Tree of Life what they deemed good and blended it with the fruit from the other tree. In the end, that other tree is what they were partaking of, and that tree renders death. Thus, His message to them is that unless they repent and turn away from this tree and spit out its fruit, He will spew them from His mouth.

This has been the problem with God's people from day one. It was the problem in the days of Elijah when he confronted Israel on Mount Carmel saying:

> "How long will you falter between two opinions? If the LORD is God, follow him; but if Baal, follow him."
>
> – 1 KINGS 18:21

In other words, "How long are you going to mix hot with cold, righteousness with unrighteousness? How long will you pick and choose what of God's Word you wish to obey?" Messiah's words are clear. If we're not going to follow Him all the way and be righteous, then we should just go ahead and be totally wicked. At least that way everyone will know what we are. In a mixed state of mind—picking and choosing—we have the appearance of being good but are actually mingled with evil, and that fruit renders death. Paul seemed to address the concept and warned us to be on guard against it.

> "But know this, that in the last days perilous times will come: For men will be lovers of themselves, lovers of money, boasters, proud, blasphemers, disobedient to parents, unthankful, unholy, unloving, unforgiving, slanderers, without self-control, brutal, despisers of good, traitors, headstrong, haughty, lovers of pleasure rather than lovers of God, having a form of godliness but denying its power. And from such people turn away! For of this sort are those who creep into households and make captives of gullible women loaded down with sins, led away by various lusts, always learning and never able to come to the knowledge of the truth."
>
> – 2 TIMOTHY 3:1-7

"Having a form of godliness but denying the power thereof" perfectly describes the Tree of the Knowledge of Good and Evil as well as the spiritual condition of the Laodiceans. It also, to some extent, describes the Church at large, and particularly in America. Here is why this is important to point out in light of our discussion: what goes on in the halls of government is a reflection of what goes on in the pews and pulpits of our churches. Still not convinced? Let's look at another passage.

In Ezekiel 20, the prophet records an event when certain elders of Israel came to him to "inquire of the LORD" (Ez. 20:1). But before they could utter a word, the LORD stopped them and began to rebuke them. He reminded them of their fathers in Egypt and how they disobeyed Him, how they complained to Him in the wilderness and how they, in general, refused to obey His Word, even though obedience would result in life (Ez. 20:11). Instead of embracing His Word —eating from the Tree of Life and living—they rebelled against Him and refused to obey His laws. Therefore, He said:

> "Because they had not executed My judgments, but had despised My statutes, profaned My Sabbaths, and their eyes were fixed on their fathers' idols. Therefore I also gave them up to statutes that were not good, and judgments by which they could not live; and I pronounced them unclean because of their ritual gifts, in that they caused all their firstborn to pass through the fire, that I might make them desolate and that they might know that I am the Lord."
>
> – Ezekiel 20:24-26

The message to His people was this: if they were not going to obey His Word, His statutes and His laws, which would result in life, then they would be turned over to laws and statutes they could not live by; laws that render death. If they were not going to eat from the Tree of Life and were going to insist on turning to the other tree, then that would, indeed, be the tree they would eat from. Reading the entire chapter, it also becomes evident that these other laws would come at the hand of oppressive governments and nations. We say that because what they came to inquire of the LORD was, "Why can't we be like all the other nations?"

> "As I live, says the Lord God, I will not be inquired of by you. What you have in your mind shall never be, when you say, 'We will be like the Gentiles, like the families in other countries, serving wood and stone.'"
>
> – Ezekiel 20:31-32

When God's people wish to be like everyone else and blend in with society, probably because we wish for everyone to like us, we cease from serving the purpose to which we were called. That purpose is to be a light to the nations; however, you cannot be a *light* to them if you are obsessed with being *like* them.

The reason Nebuchadnezzar was allowed to destroy Jerusalem and the Temple and then cart off Temple treasures to Babylon and put them in the house of his false god, was because the heart of God's people was already in Babylon. If they, in their heart, desired to mix and mingle with the nations—Babylon being the epitome of mixing and mingling—then God allowed their whole being to go to Babylon, serve the king of Babylon and be subject to his laws.

Remember, God will oftentimes give us what we want to demonstrate to us that it was not what we needed. Furthermore, if we refuse to live according to His Word and His laws and decide for ourselves what is right and what is wrong, then He will eventually turn us over to those whose laws are oppressive and change with the whims of their imagination. Therefore, if we find ourselves in a situation where the law of the land—the Constitution—is being ignored, redefined, circumvented and undermined, we suggest that it is because that is what God's people in America have done where His Word is concerned. If that is the case, should we be surprised to find that we are being subjected to oppressive laws that are, biblically speaking, lawless?

> "Then My anger shall be aroused against them in that day, and I will forsake them, and I will hide My face from them, and they shall be devoured. And many evils and troubles shall befall them,

so that they will say in that day, 'Have not these evils come upon us because our God is not among us?'"

– DEUTERONOMY 31:17

If—and we say "if"—God has hidden His face from this nation, then we should expect that His Presence will be replaced by another presence. If Winthrop's "shining city on a hill" begins to wane and retreat, the consequent power vacuum will invite every thug, despot and would-be king—domestic or otherwise—to fill it with tyranny, oppression, chaos and violence. Perhaps never in human history has there been this great a threat to freedom; one capable of extinguishing for all time, the light of liberty. In some ways, it is reminiscent of what Jesus said:

> "For then there will be great tribulation, such as has not been since the beginning of the world until this time, no, nor ever shall be. And unless those days were shortened, no flesh would be saved; but for the elect's sake those days will be shortened."

– MATTHEW 24:21-22

Yes, America and the world are entering a very dangerous hour, and as His people, we need to be the first in line to find the way that leads back to Him. We can start by abandoning the idea that we can pick and choose what part of His Word to obey and to ignore. Let's put it this way: if we redefine His laws and covenants to accommodate our lifestyle, should we then be surprised to find that the nation does likewise? If we continue to be lukewarm even as we grow "fat," our spiritual senses will be dulled, and we will continue in our apathy. The result may lead to a broken covenant.

Might it be that Samson eventually broke the covenant because years before, he had consistently broken God's commands? Essentially, he picked and chose what to honor and what to forsake, yet the Spirit of God would still come upon him. Could He have viewed God's mercy as an endorsement, causing him to let his spiritual guard down, in turn, leading to God removing the hedge of protection from around him? If we have repeated this error, should we expect the hedge that has protected us to remain?

CHAPTER EIGHT

Has the Hedge Come Down?

"Let me tell you what I will do to My vineyard; I will take away its hedge, and it shall be burned, and break down its wall, and it shall be trampled down."

– ISAIAH 5:5

T HERE IS A principle that appears in the very beginning of Scripture which teaches that, though God's people are given a privileged status — a personal relationship with the Creator of the Universe — they are also charged with a great responsibility. As for Adam, it was expressed this way:

> Then the LORD God took the man and put him in the garden of Eden to tend and keep it."
>
> – GENESIS 2:15

Put simply, the Hebrew words translated here as "to tend" and "keep" literally mean to "to work" and "to guard." This means that Adam was not only to work in the garden so that it was sustained and fruitful, but also he was to guard against anything and anyone that might come in to disrupt, contaminate and destroy the garden.

Considering the end result — man's exile from the garden — we can deduce that, though he may have tended the garden, he certainly was not diligent to guard it. How could the Adversary gain access to the midst of the garden if Adam had been committed to guard it? The point is that because of his failure to focus on the guarding aspect of his mission as well as the directive to tend the garden, a shrewd and crafty adversary infiltrated the garden, seduced the woman and subsequently enticed the man to eat of a deadly fruit.

Unfortunately, this same principle and the same error and outcome, can be found throughout the Bible and Israel's history. Again and again, they repeated the cycle of obedience that rendered blessing, followed by abuse of the blessing that rendered apathy—apathy led to rebellion—rebellion resulted in exile—and exile eventually provoked repentance, as it was meant to do. Sadly, we see this unfortunate cycle may be moving toward the rebellion phase here in America. Our prosperity has led to spiritual fatness, dulled spiritual senses and an apathetic approach to guarding against those errors which would remove our protection. When a person or a nation lets their guard down, the enemy sneaks in, burrows down deep, seduces his prey and begins to steal, kill and destroy.

For example, it is fascinating that, among other parallels that exist between the two nations, Israel and the U.S. are both being tested on their southern border. For decades now, groups like Hamas (Islamic Resistance Movement) and Hezbollah have harassed Israel's southern border and beyond with rocket attacks and incursions meant to kill as many Israelis as possible.

At the same time, the southern border of the U.S. is being overrun by those who feel that if they can get their foot in the door, they will eventually be given amnesty, which would allow them to stay and benefit as citizens without having to earn the right to obtain citizenry. One could understand their logic given the fact that the President and many in Congress have expressed intent to push for amnesty, of course, all in the name of being sympathetic to their plight.

As frustrating and debatable as the humanitarian, political and economic aspects of this situation may be, the most lethal component of it, in our opinion, has nothing to do with impoverished people trying to escape their conditions and attempt a better life in America. It has everything to do with the fact that this massive influx of foreigners provides cover for those who have a more sinister plan in mind—the violent criminals, ruthless drug lords and Islamic terrorists suspected to be among them. This scenario is neither far-fetched nor a recent development. It is something that has been going on for decades. Consider this quote from President Ronald Reagan's diary dated January 21, 1986.

> "I met with Bill Casey (CIA Director from 1981-1987) who is leaving for Saudi Arabia. I gave him word I've received that there may be some hostile actions on our Southern border and that some of the illegal Mexican entrants are actually from the Middle East."
>
> – THE REAGAN DIARIES, P. 385.

What is the position of our current administration, and what do they intend to do about the "humanitarian crisis" brewing on our southern border? The President, who we would assume has more recent information than President Reagan had decades ago, has decided to act on his own without Congressional approval. One would assume that should be interpreted as action favorable to the ten-thousands coming into America illegally rather than in favor of the Constitution and millions of Americans he is sworn to protect.

Again, the primary issue is not those who wish to escape poverty, but the many lawless among them that are coming for entirely different reasons than what is represented to us on the nightly news! It should also be pointed out that for the Administration to act in this manner, without congressional backing, is wholly unconstitutional, lawless and borders upon tyranny.

The point in all this is this: it is not sufficient just to have a productive garden, regardless of whether it is the greatest and most productive garden that the world has ever seen. If it is to continue serving its INTENDED purpose, we must also be diligent to guard and protect the garden against those who would sow tares and persuade us to eat of its deadly fruit. You see, with privileged status comes great responsibility, because in reality, "we the people" did not create the garden. Someone else did. He just allowed us to enjoy its benefits—the "blessings of liberty"—so long as we and our posterity are faithful to keep (guard) what had been entrusted to us.

We didn't plant the vineyard. He did, and He expects us to render the fruits of it in the proper season. This means that we must tend it and also guard it against those entities and philosophies that would seek to destroy it. The Republic that was entrusted to us—the one Franklin referred to—is in danger of being overrun, not by illegal aliens, but by lawlessness that is springing up from within our own borders. How did it take root and grow? Let us look to the Scripture for the answer.

> "The kingdom of heaven is likened unto a man who sowed good seed in his field: but while men slept, his enemy came and sowed tares among the wheat, and went his way. But when the grain had sprouted and produced a crop, then the tares also appeared."
>
> – MATTHEW 13:24-26

Did you catch it? The field, which is the world, contained only good seed initially. How then did it produce tares? An enemy—a *tsar*—came in and sowed a different type of seed, in fact, a deadly seed that sprung up among the wheat. The key, however, is found in this statement: "but while men slept..." If their slumber is what gave the enemy opportunity to sow this other poisonous seed in the man's field, what then, would be inferred about these men? In other words, what should they have been doing?

We will suggest that Messiah's statement implies that they should have been guarding the field, rather than sleeping. In this parable, Christ essentially tells us of mankind's fundamental problem—a tendency to relax and let our guard down, allowing the Adversary to come in. Might this deficiency within God's people be fueled by the blessings that surround us? Are we lulled to sleep by our spiritual fatness, not to mention the fatigue brought on by our constant "tending"?

While you meditate on this, consider something else. When Jesus went into the Garden of Gethsemane and left His disciples, the Bible said most of them sat in a place He directed them to. Peter, James and John went further with Him into the garden, and finally, He left them to go further still—about a stone's throw away (Luke 22:41). In a manner of speaking, He went into the midst of the garden.

When He left His disciples, it was with the instruction to "watch and pray" (Matt. 26:41). However, each time He returned to them, He found them sleeping—even as Judas and the Temple guards were on their way into the garden. Finally, Christ announced, "The spirit is indeed willing but the flesh is weak" (Matt. 26:41).

We bring this out because His directive to them was very similar to that given to Adam—"watch" meant to be "on guard." Jesus' instruction to them to "pray" would have been equivalent to God's instruction to Adam to "tend" or "till" the garden. The main point here, however, is that like the men in the parable and like Adam in the garden, at least in a spiritual sense, the disciples went to sleep as the adversary in the person of Judas was coming to bind and remove the "Tree of Life" from the midst of the garden.

This same counsel—to be on guard—was given to Israel by Moses as they prepared to enter the land of Canaan. He said:

> "Every commandment which I command you today you must be careful to observe, that you may live and multiply, and go in and possess the land of which the Lord swore to your fathers. And you shall remember that the Lord your God led you all the way these forty years in the wilderness, to humble you and test you, to know what was in your heart, whether you would keep His commandments or not. So He humbled you, allowed you to hunger, and fed you with manna which you did not know nor did your fathers know, that He might make you know that man shall not live by bread alone; but man lives by every word that proceeds from the mouth of the Lord."
>
> – DEUTERONOMY 8:1-3

The Hebrew word translated here as *observe* is the same word used when Adam is told to "keep" the garden. The Hebrew word *shamar* literally means "to guard," and according to what Moses told Israel, it was crucial that they "guard" all the commandments, not just those they chose to. If they failed to do this, they couldn't possess the land, and they could not live. They were also alerted to the fact that they could not live exclusively by the blessings God provided, physical bread, but that life was dependent on EVERY word that proceeded from the mouth of the LORD God.

We learn that there is a cost to ensure that the blessings from God continue; yes, that includes the blessings of liberty. We must do fully what He has instructed us to do. We must be equally as diligent to guard against those things that would encroach upon what He has entrusted to us, lest we be denied those blessings. If we don't remain alert and guard against spiritual threats (most often manifested in physical ways), then foreign philosophies, ideologies and "gods" will come in and rob us of the blessings God bestowed upon us. Consequently, though we may have done all the work commanded us, our failure to guard will cause us to end up like Adam—exiled from the land and cut off from God.

Moreover, if we don't work and guard **every** word—in other words, if we behave as Laodicea who picked and chose what commandments to keep—the result will be apathy and spiritual slumber. As we see throughout the Scriptures, apathy leads to broken covenants, which results in the removal of our hedge, followed by an invasion of our enemies and destruction of our life as we have known it.

Considering our nation and what has transpired in the last several years, it seems fair to say that somewhere along the way the people of America became apathetic, dozed off and left the door open for the Adversary to sow that other poisonous seed. As believers, we are admonished to, "Awake, you who sleep, arise from the dead, and Christ will give you light" (Eph. 5:14); but apparently many have remained asleep, and it would seem that we didn't "keep" or guard what was handed down to us from the Founders. We've let it slip from our grasp because we let down our guard.

Frankly, this isn't necessarily the fault of politicians, judges, bank executives, Wall Street moguls and Hollywood producers—at least not exclusively. Also, our national malady is not entirely an issue of "We the People." The real issue revolves around this phrase: "If my people." If we, the Body, fail to guard what was entrusted to us by our Father, how can we expect the nation at large to guard what He entrusted to us all? When *we* don't guard against the Adversary—if *we* are lulled to sleep—our adversaries will, indeed, come in and take root.

Allow us to accentuate that point. In the very place where William Bradford and the Pilgrims first landed, Provincetown, Massachusetts — a town promoted as "America's first Destination" — they also boast of being a "Haven of Diversity." Here is a quote taken directly from their promotional material:

> "Since the Mayflower landed here in 1620, Provincetown has built its legacy as a haven for all who seek true freedom and acceptance. P-town has become the nation's #1 destination for same-sex weddings and is a perennial top spot for numerous LGBT festivals and gatherings..."

What would Bradford and his fellow sojourners think of such a boast? Would they stand arm in arm with these people for their cause of freedom and equality? Doubtful! So, how did this happen? It is the result of His people dozing off after growing fat and apathetic and allowing the enemy to come in, stealthily at first, to sow tares in the midst of the wheat.

SATAN'S THREE-PRONGED TACTIC

Lately it seems that threats to America have been coming out of the woodwork and almost overnight. Consider the threat of Ebola, a virus that we've been aware of since the mid 1970s that is just now penetrating our borders. During the past 40 years, healthcare workers have gone to Africa to treat those afflicted and in need, and during all that time there were no reports of anyone in America being infected with the virus. However, all of a sudden, the virus is here.

Couple this with a rash of violent natural disasters over the last few years, including a three-year drought that has debilitated almost 60% of California, wreaking havoc on the agricultural industry there and having long-term ramifications for us all. On top of all that, there is the constant threat of an attack at the hands of Islamic militants. All of these issues paint a very threatening picture for America. The question is, why now? Why is this happening so suddenly? The answer may be found in the book of Job.

> "And the Lord said to Satan, 'From where do you come?' So Satan answered the Lord and said, 'From going to and fro on the earth, and from walking back and forth on it.' Then the Lord said to Satan, 'Have you considered My servant Job, that there is none like him on the earth, a blameless and upright man, one who fears God and shuns evil?' So Satan answered the Lord and said, 'Does Job fear God for nothing? Have You not made a hedge around him, around his household, and around all that he has on every side? You have blessed the work of his hands, and his possessions have increased in the land. But now, stretch out Your hand and touch all that he has, and he will surely curse You to Your face!'"

> – JOB 1:7-11

As the narrative continues, God indeed removes the hedge from around Job, giving Satan access to the man, his family and his possessions. With the hedge of protection provided by the Creator in place, Job was spared many troubles. As soon as it was removed, the Adversary was permitted to launch an all out three-pronged attack against this man who was considered the "greatest man in the east" (Job 1:3).

As the attack unfolds, one can clearly see the "steal, kill and destroy" tactics of Satan. He used foreign invaders to *steal* his property, natural disasters to *kill* his family and pestilence in an attempt to *destroy* Job. Think about it. Foreign invaders, natural disasters and disease all converged to take everything from Job with the exception of his life. Thankfully, Job held fast to his integrity and in the end, received back double what he had lost. The point, however, is to focus on the fact that during this testing, when the hedge God had placed around him was removed, everything that came against Job happened suddenly.

For years now, Americans have been alerted to the rise of Islamic terrorism and groups like ISIS, with their bold and direct threats made against the United States, including a vow to fly the flag of the Caliphate atop the White House. Now, however, we must consider the very real possibility that Islamic extremists have been crossing our southern border for decades and are poised to carry out those threats within our borders. There is also the lurking danger of home-grown terrorists and converts to Islam who sympathize with ISIS and who, like Alton Nolen of Moore, Oklahoma, are motivated to murder and behead the American "infidels" in their own homeland—in the heartland of America, no less.

Today we are faced with the threat of pestilence. In the past we've had brushes with potential epidemics and prolific disease (e.g., the bird flu), but never before has there been such a sense of foreboding doom as we have now grappling with the knowledge that the Ebola virus is in the U.S. Not since World War I and the outbreak of the Spanish Flu, which affected one in every ten homes, have we had to face the potential for a deadly pandemic. This doesn't even take into consideration the threat of other diseases which seem to be popping up out of nowhere—diseases like the Bubonic Plague.

Perhaps, and hopefully, that scenario will not play out; however, it is disturbing to see that there is no inclination whatsoever in the current administration to limit or ban travel to and from the affected regions of western Africa. That, along with there being no inclination to protect the American border from infiltration by murderers, terrorists and disease, creates potential for chaos in America in a way that has never been greater. Has the hedge come down?

Toss into the mix the fact that Nolen, an Islamic convert who murdered and beheaded a co-worker in an Oklahoma City suburb, committed his dastardly and beastly deed on Thursday, September 25, 2014. Also consider that Thomas Eric Duncan, a Liberian national and the first person to die of Ebola in the U.S., first went to a Dallas hospital sometime in the evening of Wednesday September 24, 2014, with symptoms later determined to be the Ebola virus. Comparing the timing of these two very disarming events shows that they both coincided with one of the most holy days on God's calendar, *Yom Teruah*, also known as *Rosh HaShanah*. This day is also referred to as *Yom HaDin*—Judgment Day! Was God sending us a message that our protection has been compromised?!

Just a week before this event, another disturbing and history-making event occurred for the first time in the modern era. A man was able to penetrate the protective barrier surrounding the White House (dare we say the hedge around the People's House) and enter the mansion, making it all the way to the East Room before being tackled. While no one was hurt, and some might pass it off as "no big deal," might this, along with all the other troubling events, signal that the hedge which has protected America has been or is being removed?

In regard to the White House security situation, it is worth noting that in the State Dining Room of the White House, engraved upon the mantel is a prayer attributed to President John Adams. Adams was the second president of the U.S. but was the first president to reside within the Executive Mansion. The prayer says:

> "I pray heaven to bestow the best of blessings on this house and all that shall hereafter inhabit it; may none but honest and wise men ever rule under this roof."

How fortunate we would be if that prayer had always had its intended effect, but as we surely know by now, that has not always been the case. In fact, it could be argued that God has been, to some degree, banned from the White House, and if the God of Abraham, Isaac and Jacob is no longer welcome in the "People's House," might this intruder's infiltration of what is believed to be a fortress be a message to us all? Could it be a message that the hedge has come down?

Likewise, if God is not welcome in our school houses and another presence comes in, should we be surprised to find that our schools have become war zones? If God is no longer welcome in our courthouses, should we be surprised to see that lawlessness has replaced our laws? If He is not wanted in our public squares, why would He remain in our halls of government? If the mention of God is booed at the Democratic National Convention, shouldn't we conclude that members of that entity have a disdain for Him? Why would He remain? What else can one deduce from the latest headlines but that America has collectively declared, "God is not welcome here."

Complicating this further is our leadership, both Democratic and

Republican. The current President and his team—and, yes, past administrations as well—don't seem to share the same concerns you and I have about the issues of the day. When it comes to the border, whether guarding it against would-be terrorists or deadly disease, they seem to either not believe or not care that there is a serious threat to America. The only thing anyone seems to be concerned about is the political aspect of it. While no one can really know what motivates government inaction or their general incompetence, the result still leaves Americans exposed to danger.

Some seem to think it's due to their devotion to political correctness; some say it is apathy and indifference; some believe that they actually orchestrate and welcome the insecurity and looming chaos. Whatever it is, the bottom line is that the country is in peril. Maybe it is just this simple: If God has removed His Presence, then He has taken the hedge with Him. The house has been swept out and is clean of His Holy Spirit. Consequently, the spiritual emptiness is being replaced with a presence and unclean spirit that does not have our best interest in mind.

Here, then, is what we must conclude: If groups like ISIS are not dealt with swiftly and decisively, they will make good on their threat to infiltrate America and kill as many "infidels" as they can. If the threat of pestilence, whether it is Ebola or something we have never heard of, is not taken seriously or is greeted by our leaders as a crisis that they "can't let go to waste," they'll invite an invasion of every type and sort. Then again, it might be that they are serving their God-ordained purpose—to insure that the hedge comes down.

If it has, then America can expect what we see unfold in the book of Job; a three-fold attack of foreign invaders, natural disasters and pestilence. Can you imagine what our cities will look like when people are faced with these kinds of multiple emergencies? If over 100 American cities are threatened with anarchy because a segment of society considered a Grand Jury decision to be not to their liking, as in the Ferguson, Missouri drama, how much more violence will erupt when people's lives are truly upended with all the calamities we describe here?

The potential for catastrophe, chaos, violence and death to converge

at the same time is very real. Presently, America seems to be a proverbial house of cards just waiting for a hand to swoop in and push one
card out of its place so that the whole house tumbles to the ground. In
fact, the last time America found herself in such crisis, she was a house
divided against itself, and the crisis erupted into a full-scale Civil War.

HOW THE DESTROYER GAINS ACCESS

> "Behold, therefore, I stretched out My hand against you, dimin-
> ished your allotment, and gave you up to the will of those who
> hate you..."
>
> – EZEKIEL 16:27

As is evident in the Scripture above, when a people in covenant
with God break that covenant, their hedge of protection is removed,
and they are delivered over to the will of their enemies, whether they
are external or internal foes. One thing that many Americans need to
come to grips with is that not all of our enemies live in other countries.
Many of our enemies were born and reared here and reside within our
own borders. So it was with Israel.

As they journeyed from Egypt, they were continually provoked
to complain, curse and rebel by a group among them known as the
"mixed multitude" (in Hebrew called *arav rav*). In a sense, these were
the tares sown in the midst of the wheat, so as to undermine the purpose of God for and through Israel. This is an interesting point to
consider because Paul admonished believers, specifically those in the
latter days, to take note of Israel's mistakes in the wilderness so as not
to repeat them.

> "But with most of them God was not well pleased, for their bodies
> were scattered in the wilderness. Now these things became our
> examples, to the intent that we should not lust after evil things
> as they also lusted. And do not become idolaters as were some of
> them. As it is written, 'The people sat down to eat and drink, and
> rose up to play.' Nor let us commit sexual immorality, as some of
> them did, and in one day twenty-three thousand fell; nor let us
> tempt Christ, as some of them also tempted, and were destroyed
> by serpents; nor complain, as some of them also complained, and

were destroyed by the destroyer. Now all these things happened to them as examples, and they were written for our admonition, upon whom the ends of the ages have come."

– I CORINTHIANS 10:5-11

Here are a few things we need to glean from this warning, starting with the realization that all of it was written down for our example. In other words, Paul wouldn't warn us to guard against such behavior if it were not possible that we would engage in such. Furthermore, if we were to do so, would we not expect to succumb to the same end as did those of old?

Also embedded within his warning is the fact that just because we are not native Israelis does not mean that God does not hold us to the same standard as He held them to. That means we should not allow ourselves to indulge in this kind of resistance and rebellion, thinking that He was harsh only with Israel. No, to the contrary, the Creator holds all of His covenant people to the same standard, whether they are an individual, the Body at large, or even a nation such as America that embraced the covenant with God and consented to live according to its principles.

As we have already addressed, America was founded by men and women who used the Bible to guide their lives, including how they governed and were governed. America's laws were originally, by and large, based on Judeo-Christian principles contained in the Scriptures. Our founding documents contain references, quotes and inferences taken from and linked to the Word of God. Our founders viewed this nation as a modern counterpart to biblical Israel, conceived and established by Divine providence. Consequently, the blessings, warnings and judgments pronounced upon Israel would also apply, in principle, to the United States!

It is not inconceivable, then, to expect to see the same type of issues, tendencies and maladies affecting the U.S. as was seen in ancient Israel. To add to this, if a mixed multitude was embedded in Israel as tares among the wheat, we shouldn't be surprised to find the same issue present in America. If God's purposes are represented by the wheat field, then know for certain that the Adversary will do everything he can to sow tares in that field. Israel, symbolized by the wheat, was continually bombarded by an Adversary who wanted to sow tares in the midst of God's people.

Likewise, if God ordained a particular purpose for America, rest assured the Adversary saw fit to infest this nation with a "mixed multitude" from our very beginning. Their method: to sow discord, disregard and dissension into God's field and undermine His purposes by provoking covenant people to complain, backslide and, finally, rebel. Their mission: to steal, kill and destroy.

Perhaps the most important thing to consider about Paul's warning is that those who complained about their situation—tired of manna, tired of heat, etc.—were destroyed by the Destroyer. Let's put it this way: they were destroyed in the wilderness by the very one God protected them from in Egypt!

> "For the LORD will pass through to strike the Egyptians; and when He sees the blood on the lintel, and on the two doorposts, the LORD will pass over the door, and not allow the destroyer to come in unto your houses to strike you."
>
> – EXODUS 12:23

How is it that Israel was protected from the Destroyer in Egypt but struck down by this adversary in the wilderness? In Egypt, they trusted in the blood of a lamb and applied the sign of the covenant upon their homes; they were being faithful to the covenant and were spared. In the wilderness, however, they entertained the idea that the One who had brought them out of Egypt, through the sea and to the wilderness was incapable or unwilling to bring them to the land of Promise. In short, they began to conceive their own plans, methods and goals because they listened to the voices of Korah, Dathan, Abiram and the mixed multitude.

In this comparison we see that they were spared during the initial crisis in Egypt because they trusted in God. In the subsequent crisis they were destroyed by the same threat from the first crisis because they trusted in themselves and abandoned faith in God. This is extremely important to address because we can see things taking shape today in America that may follow this same pattern. In fact, there is another example of this scenario found among the prophets — one that suggests dire consequences for our country.

THAT GREAT CITY, NINEVEH

In its heyday, Nineveh was an incredible city that started out as a mere provincial town in the time of Nimrod but eventually became the world's largest metropolis for over 50 years. At its peak, the city encompassed over three square miles, boasted of 15 gates and an elaborate system of 18 canals that brought water to over 100,000 inhabitants. That amounts to an impressive city in today's world, not to mention antiquity.

Obviously, Nineveh did not continue to be the world's greatest city. It was destroyed completely in the year 612 B.C. This sprawling city and capital of the once-great Assyrian empire, met its end, not so much at the hands of external foes but because of internal strife and civil war within its own borders. After the death of its last great king, Ashurbanipal, the empire began to unravel due to bitter and deep divides within the different factions of the empire, which included Chaldeans, Medes and others. Still, Nineveh ceased to be because, in essence, the Assyrian Empire committed suicide.

That is the official, albeit brief, history of Nineveh, but the Bible has something to say about this city that merits our attention. Before coming to its end, Nineveh was warned twice by God through two different prophets over a century apart—Jonah and Nahum. Jonah's assignment was to go to Nineveh and alert them of their impending doom forty days from his pronouncement of judgment. As we know, Jonah ran from God in an attempt to avoid this journey to Nineveh, and God used a great fish to influence Jonah to change his mind. (An interesting sidebar to this story is the belief that the word *Nineveh* is derived from the Aramaic term, *nuna*, meaning "fish.")

When the prophet finally arrived in Nineveh and warned them of their future calamity, something unexpected happened, at least as far as Jonah was concerned. They repented.

"So the people of Nineveh believed God, proclaimed a fast, and put on sackcloth, from the greatest to the least of them. Then word came to the king of Nineveh; and he arose from his throne and laid aside his robe, covered himself with sackcloth and sat in ashes. And he caused it to be proclaimed and published throughout Nineveh by the decree of the king and his nobles, saying, 'Let neither man nor beast, herd nor flock, taste anything; do not let them eat, or drink water. But let man and beast be covered with sackcloth, and cry mightily to God; yes, let everyone turn from his evil way and from the violence that is in his hands. Who can tell if God will turn and relent, and turn away from His fierce anger, so that we may not perish?'"

– JONAH 3:5-9

As the Bible records, God saw their deeds of repentance and how they turned from their evil way and, in turn, spared the city—for a while. Later, another prophet by the name of Nahum was called to pronounce a final warning against Nineveh; a city described as being a "bloody city full of lies and robbery" (Nah. 3:1). This warning was not met with the same response as before but was basically ignored. The result was the collapse of the Assyrian empire and the destruction of its greatest city as described above. Amazingly, Nahum announced his warning to Nineveh about 150 years after Jonah. Why is that amazing?

First of all, the forms of judgment pronounced upon Nineveh by Nahum were to address the same problematic tendencies we can see presently in America; problems that have divided us and have the potential to cause the nation to splinter into factions and break up. As we said earlier, the last time we faced this level of crisis was during the Civil War, about 150 years ago! Although the nation suffered, we were spared from the Destroyer in large part because of the people's response to the crisis. On the day of his second inauguration, Abraham Lincoln acknowledged that the crisis was the handiwork of God.

"If we shall suppose that American slavery is one of those offenses which, in the providence of God, must needs come, but which, having continued through His appointed time, He now wills to remove, and that He gives to both North and South this terrible war as the woe due to those by whom the offense came, shall we discern therein any departure from those divine attributes which the believers in a living God always ascribe to Him? Fondly do we hope, fervently do we pray, that this mighty scourge of war may speedily pass away. Yet, if God wills that it continue until all the wealth piled by the bondsman's two hundred and fifty years of unrequited toil shall be sunk, and until every drop of blood drawn with the lash shall be paid by another drawn with the sword, as was said three thousand years ago, so still it must be said "the judgments of the LORD are true and righteous altogether."

— ABRAHAM LINCOLN

Assyria was spared at first. But eventually the sins became so great that their refusal to repent removed any barrier that protected them from destruction. Just before the end, history tells us that a new Assyrian king formed a neo-Assyrian Empire. However, that quickly dissolved into civil war, internal strife, neighbor pitted against their neighbor, and philosophy warring against philosophy until, eventually, Babylonians and Medes pulled them down altogether.

The Civil War could have destroyed America but it didn't. Yet, the internal strife we see today has direct relationship to what was addressed 150 years ago. Repentance and faith in the Almighty is what averted disaster then, but will we see that same response as this latest crisis develops? Frankly, it is hard to imagine that we will when our nation is filled with the innocent blood of 50 *million* abortion victims. It is hard to imagine a spirit of repentance overtaking us as it did in Nineveh when our nation's leaders are compelled to deceive and manipulate the American people in order to get elected or get a law pushed through. For decades now we have been warned, but so few seem to be paying attention! In reality, the nation is already divided and splintered into so many different factions that only the grace of God prevents us from collapsing.

In the mid 19th century, the conflict was over slavery and states' rights; the battle lines were drawn between North and South. Today, the battle is between cultures, ideologies and what is right and what is wrong. The lines of battle are drawn in most every community throughout the nation. Couple our distressing internal affairs with the fact that, externally, we are facing looming crises with the Islamic radicals in Iraq and the mullahs in Iran, which are ironically the descendants of the same people God used to inflict the *coup de grâce* upon the city of Nineveh and the Assyrian empire!

Is God's protection over us being lifted? Are we slowly edging toward our own self-inflicted destruction? Only time will tell, but this we know: if the hedge is being removed, many will suffer at unprecedented levels and in ways not thought possible in America. Furthermore, because we have been in covenant with the Creator, the entire world will be allowed to observe the outcome and be struck with awe at what befalls us. Two thousand years ago, Christ warned the men of Capernaum (ironically the "village of Nahum") that the people of Sodom would have repented had they witnessed what the people of Capernaum had seen; yet, Capernaum did not repent and was later destroyed. Jesus also warned those of that same generation that:

> "The men of Nineveh shall rise in the judgment with this generation and condemn it, because they repented at the preaching of Jonah; and indeed a greater than Jonah is here. The Queen of the South will rise up in the judgment with this generation and condemn it, for she came from the ends of the earth to hear the wisdom of Solomon; and indeed a greater than Solomon is here."
>
> – MATTHEW 12:41-42

If we don't repent, the same will be said of us. The Queen of the South will rise in judgment; Sodom and Nineveh will also rise in judgment against this wicked and adulterous generation if we do not repent. If that happens, we will only have ourselves to blame because, for all eternity, God is just. Frankly, this frightening scenario sounds strikingly similar to something else recorded in Scripture.

> "So Pharaoh rose in the night, he, all his servants, and all the Egyptians; and there was a great cry in Egypt, for there was not a house where there was not one dead."
>
> – EXODUS 12:30

Might it come to this for America if her hedge has been removed? Let us pray not! Rather than being dismayed, as believers we should be reminded that Job held fast to his integrity and endured the trial he was subjected to. In the end he was restored and given twice what he had lost. We should also remember the promise contained in this Scripture we cited earlier.

> "The Lord will pass through to strike the Egyptians; and when He sees the blood on the lintel and on the two doorposts, the Lord will pass over the door and not allow the destroyer to come into your houses to strike you."
>
> – EXODUS 12:23

HOLD FAST TO YOUR INTEGRITY

Though we, like Job and so many others, may have to endure a fiery trial, if we hold fast to our integrity, place our confidence in Him and trust in the blood of the Lamb then...

> "Surely He shall deliver you from the snare of the fowler and from the perilous pestilence. He shall cover you with His feathers, and under His wings you shall take refuge; His truth shall be your shield and buckler. You shall not be afraid of the terror by night, nor of the arrow that flies by day, nor of the pestilence that walks in darkness, nor of the destruction that lays waste at noonday. A thousand may fall at your side and ten thousand at your right hand; but it shall not come near you. Only with your eyes shall you look and see the reward of the wicked. Because you have made the Lord, who is my refuge, even the Most High, your dwelling place. No evil shall befall you, nor shall any plague come near your dwelling."
>
> – PSALM 91:3-10

As believers, it is extremely important that we hold fast to these promises because if America and the world continue upon the path we are currently on, eventually God will separate those who are His from those who are not. Make no doubt about it, a separation is coming in advance of the looming destruction. The evidence of this is seen throughout the Scripture beginning with Israel's impending departure from Egypt. As God prepared to pour out the last seven plagues upon Egypt, He said to Pharaoh:

> "And in that day I will set apart the land of Goshen, in which my people dwell, that no swarms of flies shall be there; in order that you may know that I am the LORD in the midst of the land. I will make a difference between my people and your people: Tomorrow this sign shall be."
>
> — EXODUS 8:22-23

The Hebrew root word translated here as "difference" is *palah* and means "separate, sever or distinguish." God wished to distinguish His people from the Egyptians by preserving them from the trouble that was coming, and here's the main reason why: so that the Egyptians would know that "I am the LORD." Interestingly, the word *palah* also means "make wonderful" and is the root of the word found in the book of Judges when the angel describes his name to Manoah, Samson's father, as "wonderful."

> "And the angel of the LORD said unto him, 'Why do you ask my name, seeing it is wonderful?'"
>
> — JUDGES 13:18

What might we glean from this? Those who deny the existence of God or who deny His authority over their lives or their nation will eventually change their tune when calamities befall them at every turn. They will, willingly or begrudgingly, acknowledge His power and sovereignty over all nations, and He will be regarded as the One and only God, distinguished from the gods of the nations. He alone is "wonderful." Even Pharaoh, with his hardened heart, and all of his advisors eventually conceded that the God of Israel was God (Ex. 9:27, 10:7). As it is written:

> "At the name of Jesus every knee should bow, of those in heaven, and of those on earth, and of those under the earth, and that every tongue should confess that Jesus Christ is Lord, to the glory of God the Father."
>
> — PHILIPPIANS 2:10-11

In Egypt, God brought Pharaoh and his counselors to this point by setting a distinction between His people and everyone else so all would see that the judgments pronounced upon Egypt served simultaneously as vindication for Israel. By distinguishing them from Egypt, He did not conceal them from the Egyptians. To the contrary, He caused them to stand out as a beacon shining in the darkness so that friend and foe alike would have to conclude that the God of Israel has the power to destroy and the power to save with the same act.

> "And the LORD will make a difference between the livestock of Israel and the livestock of Egypt. So nothing shall die of all that belongs to the children of Israel. Then the LORD appointed a set time, saying, 'Tomorrow the LORD will do this thing in the land.' So the LORD did this thing on the next day, and all the livestock of Egypt died: but of the livestock of the children of Israel, not one died."
>
> – Exodus 9:4-6

> "And the hail struck throughout the whole land of Egypt, all that was in the field, both man and beast; and the hail struck every herb of the field, and broke every tree of the field. Only in the land of Goshen, where the children of Israel were, there was no hail."
>
> – Exodus 9:25-26

When God causes it to rain on the just and the unjust, consider that for the just it is a blessing; for the unjust it might be a curse. Likewise, when He pours out judgment, for the unjust it may prove to be a punishment while, at the same time, it may be vindication for the just. Where Egypt was concerned the hedge was removed from the nation, yet God continued to protect His people in the midst of the calamity so that Israel AND Egypt would know that He alone is the LORD.

If He did this 3,500 years ago, He can—and we believe He will—do it again. In fact, the Scripture is not only replete with examples of how God protected His people from judgments in times past, including those like Lot who were spared because of the prayers of the righteous, but Scripture also makes clear He will distinguish and deliver His people in the last days. Christ makes this very clear in multiple parables.

For example, in Matthew 13 the tares are removed from the field to be burned, leaving the wheat to be gathered into the owner's barn. Messiah makes it clear that this reveals how the sons of the wicked one will be destroyed, and the sons of the kingdom will be saved at the end of days (Mat. 13:39-40). In Matthew 25, Jesus says that at His coming all peoples will be as sheep and goats gathered before Him. Yet, He separates the sheep from the goats and allows the sheep into the Kingdom while the goats are sent away from Him into punishment (Mat. 25:33-41). In yet another example He said:

> "Again, the kingdom of heaven is like a dragnet that was cast into the sea, and gathered some of every kind, which, when it was full, they drew to shore, and they sat down and gathered the good into vessels, but threw the bad away. So it will be at the end of the age. The angels will come forth, separate the wicked from among the just, and cast them into the furnace of fire. There shall be wailing and gnashing of teeth."
>
> – MATTHEW 13:47-50

These examples not only demonstrate what is going to happen at the end of the age when He comes to rule and reign, they also demonstrate the principle we have been discussing. God sets a distinction between His people and those of the world, sparing His people the calamities that befall others while, at the same time, using their preservation to testify to those in darkness. Consider what Jesus told the congregation at Philadelphia:

> "I know your works. See, I have set before you an open door, and no one can shut it: for you have a little strength, have kept my word, and have not denied my name. Indeed, I will make those of the synagogue of Satan, which say they are Jews, and are not, but lie — indeed, I will make them come and worship before your feet, and to know that I have loved you. Because you have kept my command to persevere, I also will keep you from the hour of trial which shall come upon the whole world, to test those who dwell on the earth."
>
> – REVELATION 3:8-10

If those of Philadelphia and those they represent in the last days are preserved from the trial befalling all others, might it be for the same reason that He set a distinction between Israel and the Egyptians—so that all will know that He is the LORD? In other words, He makes His people to be a "city set upon a hill." As Christ said:

> "You are the light of the world. A city that is set on a hill cannot be hidden. Nor do they light a lamp, and put it under a basket, but on a lampstand and it gives light to all who are in the house. Let your light so shine before men, that they may see your good works, and glorify your Father in heaven."
>
> – MATTHEW 5:14-16

So then, if the hedge has come down and an all-out attack is to commence against this nation bringing down all that men have set their affections on—wealth, power, sex, etc.—that doesn't mean that we are to cease from our purpose. We are commanded to occupy until He comes, to let our light shine even in the midst of the darkness and to allow our Heavenly Father to set a distinction between us and the world. It seems rather fitting that 400 years later we are again being reminded to be what John Winthrop envisioned for all of America as he sailed toward the New World—"a shining city set upon a hill."

It makes perfect sense because God's purposes for His people have not changed even though, unfortunately, His people have. As He purposed for Israel in Egypt long ago, He intends for us today; to set a distinction between us and the world that all, friend and foe alike, may observe what He does in our lives to the glory of His Name, even as the darkness descends.

> "So Moses stretched out his hand toward heaven, and there was thick darkness in all the land of Egypt three days. They did not see one another; nor did anyone rise from his place for three days. But all the children of Israel had light in their dwellings."
>
> – EXODUS 10:22-23

The people of America have cried out for change, and change is what they shall have. A very dramatic change is coming and especially if God has removed the hedge that has protected this nation thus far. That should not cause us to shutter in fear, nor should it cause us to gloat or take joy in the inevitable judgment that comes with this change. To the contrary, the Creator takes no pleasure in the destruction of the wicked and neither should we. Considering the hour, it is imperative that we let our light shine as never before.

That is what we, as believers, must do as we see the change and transition coming. Furthermore, we must appeal to our Father in Heaven that He would be merciful to us and deliver us from what is coming upon the earth. When Israel cried out to God in Egypt, He heard their groaning and "remembered the covenant with Abraham, Isaac and Jacob" (Ex. 2:23-24). It is also in our best interest to cry out on behalf of our nation and, as we are commanded, to pray for our leaders, because unless the nation is repentant, more change and more transition is yet to come!

CHAPTER NINE

Changing of the Guard

"At that time Michael shall stand up, the great
prince who stands watch over the sons of your people;
and there shall be a time of trouble, such as never
was since there was a nation, even to that time.
And at that time your people shall be delivered,
everyone who is found written in the book."

— DANIEL 12:1

THE BOOK OF Daniel, perhaps more than any other book in the Bible, reveals critical information about spiritual warfare between the angels of God and demonic powers, as well as how God orchestrates events intended to raise up and bring down nations. Moreover, every event in the lives of nations—whoever they may be—is a link in the chain of events intended to bring about God's purpose for His people. For instance, in the passage above Michael stands guard over the people of Israel to protect them during the world's worst time of distress. (By the way, the Hebrew word "distress" is *tzarah*, the root for *tzar*—"enemy").

Also notice that certain angels and principalities are assigned to different nations. As we see, Michael is assigned to protect Israel, but we also learn that there are angelic princes over Persia and Greece (Dan. 10:20). Not only are these princes assigned to their particular nation, apparently these angels and princes know and respect the boundaries that have been established for those nations by God, who did so in regard to how it would impact the nation of Israel.

> "When the most High divided their inheritance to the nations; when He separated the sons of Adam, He set the boundaries of the peoples according to the number of the children of Israel."
>
> – Deuteronomy 32:8

The Septuagint—the Greek translation of the Hebrew text—reads slightly different. It says:

> "He established the bounds of the nations according to the number of angels of God."

Why is this important to our narrative here? If there is a contest being fought on earth, in our case a fight for the heart and soul of America, then rest assured there is a heavenly struggle being waged as well. Furthermore, the Scripture is clear that, depending on the outcome of this heavenly battle, powers and empires will rise and fall; those in power will succumb to those who are rising to power. For example, the Medes and Persians overthrew the once invincible Babylonians in one night!

Also, when this shift in power occurs, it will further the purpose of God where Israel is concerned. For instance, history records that it was Persia's Cyrus the Great who built the Medo-Persian Empire and who vanquished Babylon. According to Scripture, it was that same Cyrus, moved upon by God, who issued a decree that the Jews return to Judea and rebuild the Temple in Jerusalem.

> "Now in the first year of Cyrus king of Persia, that the Word of the LORD by the mouth of Jeremiah might be fulfilled, the LORD stirred up the spirit of Cyrus king of Persia, so that he made a proclamation throughout all his kingdom, and also put it in writing, saying, 'Thus says Cyrus king of Persia: all the kingdoms of the earth the LORD God of heaven has given me. And He has commanded me to build Him a house at Jerusalem, which is in Judah. Who is among you of all His people? May the LORD his God be with him, and let him go up.'"
>
> – 2 Chronicles 36:22-23

Josephus recorded that Cyrus was moved to do this because someone in Babylon—some traditions say Daniel—brought a 150 year-old prophecy from Isaiah to his attention.

> (The LORD) Who says of Cyrus, 'He is My shepherd, and he shall perform all My pleasure, saying to Jerusalem, "You shall be built," and to the temple, "Your foundation shall be laid."'
>
> – ISAIAH 44:28

Still, it was years later under the rule of Darius the Mede, that the decree was ultimately carried out. In fact, it seems that there was a bit of trepidation on the king's part to release the Jews to do this, but as reported by an angel to Daniel, "I stood to confirm and to strengthen him" (Dan 11:1). Why did it take so long? Because God had determined a set time for this to occur, and it happened just as He intended.

The angel's acknowledgment that Darius was strengthened by a heavenly force that provoked him to act strongly suggests that God uses these heavenly messengers to carry out His purposes through nations and kings, as well as His decisions concerning the status of those nations and kings. Keep in mind that all these decisions are engineered to further His overall plan for His people, Israel. When the foreordained time for a particular nation has come to an end, the decree is implemented by angels who move upon the land, its people and other related factors. Consequently, the principality that was granted a season and assigned to that particular nation is also vanquished, allowing another nation and its appointed principality to rise and assume the position just vacated by the former. The book of Daniel provides an example.

> "Then he said, 'Do you know why I have come to you? And now I must return to fight with the prince of Persia: and when I have gone forth, indeed the prince of Greece will come."
>
> – DANIEL 10:20

This angel was sent by God to Daniel to foretell of what would happen to his people in the latter days, however, he was resisted by the "prince of the kingdom of Persia" (Dan. 10:13). Most likely his resistance was related to what would be revealed in the angelic message, namely, a determined end to his power on earth. Apparently, this angel was sent—with the help of Michael, guardian angel of Israel—to vanquish the prince of Persia so that the prince of Greece could rise to power.

History records that, indeed, Alexander and the Greeks overran the Persians and established a Hellenistic empire stretching from Western Europe into India. As the empire spread, so did Greek culture and philosophy, including humanism and their unique brand of idolatry. Still, this had been decreed by God and would, in time, advance His plan for the people of Israel—and it was carried out by angels.

Why is all of this information important to us? Again, it demonstrates that every nation and every king rises and falls because of what God has determined. Even Nebuchadnezzar, king of Babylon, who destroyed Jerusalem and the Temple and carted off the holy treasures to place them in the house of his god, is called by God, "my servant" (Jeremiah 25:9). All things are done to perform His will. Incredible as it may seem, even the Beast of Revelation and the season in which he rises has been foreordained by God in order that *His* purposes are fulfilled.

> "The ten horns which you saw are ten kings who have received no kingdom as yet, but they receive authority for one hour as kings with the beast. These are of one mind, and they will give their power and authority to the beast.... And the ten horns which you saw on the beast, these will hate the harlot, make her desolate and naked, eat her flesh, and burn her with fire. For God has put it into their hearts to fulfill His purpose, to be of one mind, and to give their kingdom to the beast, until the words of God are fulfilled."
>
> – REVELATION 17:12-13, 16-17

Yes, all kingdoms, nations and countries—including the United States—were for a purpose and were determined a season to rise and fall because in the end, all kingdoms will become "the kingdoms of our Lord and of His Christ" (Rev. 11:15). Based upon what we have seen in Scripture, the rise and fall of these kingdoms are physical manifestations of what was first being played out in the heavens. Thus we can conclude that the obvious contest raging in America today is because of a contest raging in the spiritual realm, indicating that, most likely, a transition of power is at hand.

WHEN GOD LIFTS HIS HAND

> "Now see that I, even I, am He, and there is no God besides Me; I kill and I make alive; I wound and I heal, nor is there any who can deliver from My hand. For I raise My hand to heaven and say, 'As I live forever, if I whet My glittering sword and My hand takes hold on judgment, I will render vengeance to My enemies and repay those who hate Me. I will make My arrows drunk with blood, and My sword shall devour flesh, with the blood of the slain and the captives, from the heads of the leaders of the enemy.'"
>
> – DEUTERONOMY 32:39-42

With change, unfortunately for America, comes transition from superpower to—well, that's anyone's guess. We do know, however, that if America is waning in power and influence, that means another kingdom is on the rise. If America is being mocked and scorned rather than being feared and respected, the people of the world will notice it long before most Americans will be willing to accept it. Isn't it odd that those who used to live under the iron fist of Communism are the ones warning us that what they witnessed in the Soviet Union is happening now in the United States?

There are voices in America, those who left the socialist states in Europe to come here seeking opportunity, who are warning us that we are now succumbing to the lure of the failed philosophies of socialism. There are even those who survived Hitler's Germany, now living in America, that are suggesting that events unfolding here today are exactly like those early days of Nazi Germany when Hitler seized control of banks, the auto industry and healthcare!

There is, without doubt, a transition occurring in America, and that means that the spirit of liberty is being usurped by some other spirit. If there has been, heretofore, an angel assigned to bring about the rise and greatness of America, might it be that this angel is being vanquished by another—one that will usher in some other strong man and powerful nation intent on our destruction? If so, can we discern the identity of that spirit and principality? Consider a few possibilities as revealed in the book of Revelation.

> "The light of a lamp shall not shine in you anymore, and the voice of the bridegroom and of the bride shall not be heard in you anymore; for your merchants were the great men of the earth; for by your sorceries all the nations were deceived."
>
> – REVELATION 18:23

As a nation that has long considered itself to be, and has been considered by others to be, a light among the nations, it is hard **not** to notice that the recipient of this judgment will no longer have light and will not be a light. For America's fathers and founders, were they here to comment, this outcome would be the ultimate catastrophe for their beloved country. Is God, in fact, speaking to America here? Let us look deeper.

Her "merchants *were* the great men of the earth." Just recently, New York City was surpassed by London as the greatest city on earth in regard to wealth, investments and marketing; not to mention the preferred destination for the rich and famous to set up shop. More and more, the financial stability of the United States is being challenged and questioned by other global economic powers. For instance, a substantial and concerted effort is being made by various nations to replace the dollar as the world's de facto currency.

When it comes to our resources and industries, those are quickly being acquired by foreign investors. "American made" no longer means it is "American owned." If it comes out of Detroit it might be owned by Arab investors; Hawaii is being bought out by Japanese merchants, while New York and Californian interests are being scooped up by the emerging Chinese wealth. This buyout of American corporations and resources is more than just a sign of a global economy; it is a sign of God's displeasure. As a consequence of Israel's failure to keep the covenant with God, He said:

> "The alien who is among you shall rise higher and higher above you, and you shall come down lower and lower. He shall lend to you, but you shall not lend to him; he shall be the head, and you shall be the tail."
>
> – DEUTERONOMY 28:43-44

This certainly seems to describe America considering that our youth are falling behind in math and science skills, dropping to levels associated with third-world nations. Our technology, including technology of a military nature, is being stolen by rogue countries, reproduced and used against us. Other nations are developing their own technology and are usurping our role as a leader in most technical fields.

More and more, our citizens are dependent upon government assistance because jobs have either been shipped overseas or are being crippled under the weight of government regulation. Either way, it is propagating a dependent mentality that is not producing anything in the marketplace. All we seem to have left is an abundance of land that can be developed for food. The problem there is, as we just stated, that resource is being bought up by those who wish us no good will. So have we become the tail—a byword among the nations?

There are some exports that America still excels at, perhaps even hinted of in the verse from Revelation 18 we cited above. In that verse, the great merchants of Babylon distributed another type of commodity, if you can call it that—sorcery. Though the word could suggest witchcraft and the like, the Greek term is *pharmakeia* and is the word from which we derive our words *pharmacy* and *pharmaceuticals*— in other words, drugs! Whether it is street drugs like meth and crack or prescription drugs such as Xanax or Prozac, Americans have an obvious addiction problem which is enthusiastically exported to other countries.

There are reportedly 22 million addicts in the USA alone, and only an estimated 11% are getting any kind of treatment. That means that 89%—19.5 million people—are slowly killing themselves, and many of them with legal permission. In fact, pharmaceuticals are alleged to be the second leading cause of unintentional death in the U.S. And if we can't get a prescription for our drug of choice because it is illegal,

we compel our legislatures to make it legal, as in the case of marijuana. To date, medical and recreational use of marijuana is legal in
four western states and the District of Columbia; Florida also legalized medical use of marijuana. In short, we are now legalizing street
drugs in order to fill our tax coffers.

Since recreational pot has been legalized in Colorado, more and
more transients and those in need of government assistance are
showing up in Colorado cities and placing a drain on the public funds.
It is not too difficult to see what this is eventually going to lead to—
utter chaos. This is just *one* addiction—there are many others such as
alcohol, pornography and sex—but collectively they should cause us to
consider whether our addictive nature is merely a sign of weakness or a
sign of God's displeasure. Remember, just as God gave Israel the quail
they desired until it was coming out of their nostrils, He continues to
give people want they want to demonstrate to them it is not what they
need. As a nation we have pursued vices until now it is coming out of
our collective noses and threatening the very life of our country.

While the argument could be successfully prosecuted that, to some
degree, these kinds of issues have always existed in America, most
would have to concede that these were not the issues America was
known for throughout most of her history. More than exporting pornography and drugs, America was known for exporting liberty, hope
and, most importantly, the Gospel of the Kingdom. So, obviously
things have changed significantly, and that means a transition of some
sort is in process; but it gets worse.

SHEDDING INNOCENT BLOOD

There are other issues to consider, some of which are inferred in
Deuteronomy 32 when God says:

> "I will render vengeance to my enemies... He will avenge
> the blood of his servants, and will render vengeance to his
> adversaries..."

> – DEUTERONOMY 32:41, 43

Those who identify themselves as His enemy—opposing Him, His Word and His purposes —are promised vengeance along with those who shed the blood of His servants; some of whom were incapable of defending themselves such as the innocent unborn. We certainly do not need to expound upon the horrors of abortion, infanticide, the euthanizing of the helpless like Terri Schiavo or elderly genocide, but we will call special attention to God's response to those guilty of such atrocities.

> "I will set My face against that man and will cut him off from his people, because he has given some of his descendants to Molech, to defile My sanctuary and profane My holy name. And if the people of the land should in any way hide their eyes from the man when he gives some of his descendants to Molech, and they do not kill him, then I will set My face against that man and against his family; and I will cut him off from his people, and all who prostitute themselves with him to commit harlotry with Molech."
>
> – LEVITICUS 20:3-5

In other words, if a community or nation will not step in and stop people from willfully slaughtering their own children for whatever the reason or belief, God will cut off that person, that community and that nation; they have, in a sense, slept with a false and bloodthirsty god. No one is exempt from this warning; in fact, Christ pronounced judgment upon Jerusalem, the very city of the King, because they had shed innocent blood.

> "Therefore, indeed, I send you prophets, wise men and scribes; some of them you will kill and crucify, and some of them you will scourge in your synagogues and persecute from city to city, that on you may come all the righteous blood shed on the earth, from the blood of righteous Abel to the blood of Zechariah the son of Berechiah, whom you murdered between the sanctuary and the altar. Assuredly, I say to you, all these things will come upon this generation. O Jerusalem, Jerusalem, the one that kills the prophets and stones those who are sent to her! How often I wanted to gather your children together as a hen gathers her

chicks under her wings, but you were not willing! See! Your house is left to you desolate."

– Matthew 23:34-38

Within one generation of Christ's statement regarding Jerusalem, the Jewish capital was surrounded by the Roman 10th Legion. After a lengthy siege, Roman forces eventually penetrated the massive stone walls and reduced the once beautiful city to ashes. Not even the Temple, regarded as God's House, was spared from the destruction. Roman soldiers looted the holy vessels and carted away the gold and silver treasures and eventually paraded them through the streets of Rome as spoils of war. For the citizens of Jerusalem it was beyond devastating. Thousands of men, women and children were slaughtered and tens of thousands were carried away in chains never to see their beloved homeland again. Why did all of this happen? Because rather than turning from their sin, they chose to shed the blood of innocents.

When innocent blood is poured onto the ground through an act of murder, such as when Cain slaughtered righteous Abel, the victim's blood cries unto God from the ground (Gen. 4:10). In Revelation 6, the martyred saints cry out to God asking, "How long... until you judge and avenge our blood?" (Rev. 6:10). It would seem that the blood of innocent victims cries out to God from the ground for vengeance upon the guilty. Imagine then, how the sound of 50 million innocent voices crying unto God from the soil of America must grieve His heart and kindle His fury.

Since 1973, when the US Supreme Court legalized abortion, clinics across our nation have legally slaughtered these innocent and defenseless victims within their mother's wombs. Oftentimes, the tattered remains of these priceless little ones are discarded as if they were nothing more than household garbage. If He did not spare Jerusalem—the city of the great King (Ps.48:2)—for the shedding of innocent blood, what price might America expect to pay for the innocent blood on our hands?

The concept is simple: God made mankind in His image and likeness and breathed the breath of life into him. He declared that "the life of all flesh is in the blood" (Lev. 17:11) and determined that those who shed innocent blood—those who deny others their life—are murderers and worthy of death. You see, the God of Israel is "not God of the dead, but of the living" (Lk. 20:38). Therefore, anyone who opposes life opposes Him; if they are enemies to life they are enemies to God and are exposed and subjected to His vengeance. That reality brings to mind another example of the anti-life spirit permeating our culture today; one that parades around the country under the banner of "love" and "equality."

THE DAYS OF LOT AND NOAH

> "As it was in the days of Noah, so will it be also in the days of the Son of Man. They ate, they drank, they married wives, they were given in marriage, until the day that Noah entered the ark, and the flood came, and destroyed them all. Likewise as it was also in the days of Lot; they ate, they drank, they bought, they sold, they planted, they built; but on the day that Lot went out of Sodom it rained fire and brimstone from heaven and destroyed them all. Even so will it be in the day when the Son of man is revealed."
>
> – LUKE 17:26-30

As we have stated before, to wholly understand the events of today and tomorrow, we must first examine and understand the events of the past. Messiah tells us here that we will be able to recognize the day and season of His coming by going back and looking at what happened in the days of Noah and Lot.

The days of Noah are exemplified, more than anything else, by mixing—that is, mixing what is holy with what is profane. When the sons of God took wives for themselves from among the daughters of men, they were, in effect, mingling what was to be holy with what was common. In a manner of speaking, mankind had reproduced the tree of which God told man not to eat—the Knowledge of Good and Evil. The result was the same as in the Garden; in the end, God lamented the fact that He had made man and determined to destroy everything that moved upon the earth. Because good seed had been mingled with bad seed, it was necessary for Him to flood His field (the world) to rid it of all the corruptible seed.

Today we see this same principle in several areas of life. One way that is evident to most is how our food is being genetically manipulated in order to produce a sustainable food supply (or at least that is what is being presented to the masses.) Actually, the opposite is what it leads to. Because mankind has now taken the seed God created for food and mingled it with things God never intended for food, we are facing mounting health problems and one day, a crash of our food supply. In other words, though it appeared to be for a good cause, mankind is "creating" and eating "food" that is killing us in a most literal sense.

Alarming though that may be, we would argue that this problem is merely the reflection of a much larger problem. This physical corruption is occurring because of an ongoing spiritual malady. Put simply, the real issue of the day is not what science is doing to our daily bread but what those who are supposed to be the sons of God are doing with the Bread of Life—the Word of God.

In this day and time, there are many in the Body of Messiah who are taking the Word of God—the Good Seed (Lk. 8:11)—and mingling it with the philosophies of men, the corruptible seed. They are mixing sound biblical doctrine with false doctrine, the result being the same deadly fruit that led to man's downfall in the beginning. In effect, this is the spiritual equivalent of what science is doing to our food with the development of GMOs (Genetically Modified Organisms); in this case, men are genetically modifying God's Word. Paul said that this day would come.

> "Now the Spirit expressly says that in latter times some will depart from the faith, giving heed to deceiving spirits and doctrines of demons, speaking lies in hypocrisy, having their own conscience seared with a hot iron."
>
> – 1 Timothy 4:1-2

This verse, along with other similar warnings, testifies to Christ foretelling that the latter days are just as the beginning; the sons of God are again mating themselves to things—ideas, philosophies, etc.—that are profane and unclean. Just like the sons of God in the beginning whose offspring (fruit) hastened the death and destruction of the Flood, our mixed spiritual fruit renders death when the world is in desperate need of life. In a very significant way, the Body of Christ is responsible for the fact that few outside the remnant of true believers know for sure what truth and holiness really look like.

As a whole, we have become the Laodicean congregation that Jesus warned to repent; we have become those He told to cease being lukewarm and mixed, lest we continue producing fruit that makes Him sick. Though it appears good and healthy to us and the world, in reality it yields death, and He is not God of the dead but of the living.

Anything that renders death cannot produce life; death is the result of the other seed that God warned us not to partake of. Anything that renders death is in opposition to God and His Word. As we discussed earlier, anything that is in opposition to God, His Word and His purpose is essentially His enemy and will eventually be destroyed in the day of His vengeance. In that vein, let us now examine the days of Lot and what they teach of the days just before the Messiah returns.

THE SIN OF SODOM

When we hear the word Sodom and consider what became of this wicked city and the other cities of the plain, one grievous sin comes to mind, first and foremost. Society even coined a word — sodomy — that described these perverted acts to remind us of what happens to those who engage in such activity. However, we might be surprised to discover that, even though God punished them for this lifestyle, there were other contributing factors to Sodom's destruction.

> "Look, this was the iniquity of your sister Sodom: She and her daughter had pride, fullness of food, and abundance of idleness; neither did she strengthen the hand of the poor and needy. And they were haughty and committed abomination before Me; therefore I took them away as I saw fit."
>
> – EZEKIEL 16:49-50

The first thing the Creator accused them of was pride; the kind of pride that provokes a person to ignore the instructions of the Creator and to do what is right in his own eyes. In fact, pride will convince one that there is no God.

> "The wicked boasts of the desires of his soul, and the one greedy for gain curses and renounces the LORD. In the pride of his face the wicked does not seek him; all his thoughts are, 'There is no God.'"
>
> — PSALM 10:3-4 (ESV)

If there is no God, then there are no absolutes when it comes to good and evil, right and wrong. As a result, there are no consequences, and it becomes convenient for man to redefine the reality of natural law to accommodate his desired lifestyle.

The second issue raised in regard to Sodom's destruction was "fullness of food." Obviously, being situated in a fertile plain that Moses described as being like "the garden of the LORD, like the land of Egypt" (Gen. 13:10), Sodom and the cities of the plain would have had an abundance of food and, presumably, that would have resulted in a lot of "fat" people. How does having a full belly lead to such wickedness as associated with Sodom? Let's go back to something the Creator warned Israel of before they crossed the Jordan into the land of Canaan.

> "When I have brought them to the land flowing with milk and honey, of which I swore to their fathers, and they have eaten and filled themselves and grown *fat*, then they will turn to other gods and serve them; and they will provoke Me and break My covenant."
>
> — DEUTERONOMY 31:20

Also, recall what the unnamed prophet told Eli, the apathetic High Priest of Israel.

> "Why do you kick at My sacrifice and My offering which I have commanded in My dwelling place, and honor your sons more than Me, to make yourselves *fat* with the best of all the offerings of Israel My people?'
>
> — 1 SAMUEL 2:29

It would seem that "fullness of food"—something intended to be a blessing—can be a curse; it can lead to poverty and rags (Pro. 23:21) and also a lack of spiritual keenness and sensitivity. Apparently, in times past, that lack of spiritual sensitivity led people to engage in other indulgences; things far more wicked than eating too much at your favorite restaurant. Apparently an abundance of food—getting fat—leads to idolatry and abandoning the covenant with the God of Israel.

Another of Sodom's detriments was their "abundance of idleness"—having too much time on their hands. You know the old saying, "an idle mind is the devil's workshop." Well, apparently that was and is true. Having all that idle time on their hands was not a good combination for those who were already guilty of pride and gluttony. It gave them ample opportunity to devise more wicked schemes. It may have also contributed to their lack of compassion and consideration for those less fortunate than they, thus the accusation, "neither did she strengthen the hand of the poor and needy."

Inferred within this particular accusation is the precept concerning a "false balance"—something the Creator finds to be abominable. Here are some Scriptures to explain.

> "A false balance is abomination to the LORD: but a just weight is his delight."
>
> – PROVERBS 11:1 (KJV)

> "Diverse weights are an abomination unto the LORD and a false balance is not good."
>
> – PROVERBS 20:23 (KJV)

> "You shall not have in your bag differing weights, a heavy and a light. You shall not have in your house differing measures, a large and a small. You shall have a perfect and just measure that your days may be lengthened in the land which the LORD your God is giving you."
>
> – DEUTERONOMY 25:13-15

The Hebrew word translated "false" is *mirmah* and means "to be deceitful, to be fraudulent." Thus, a false balance is one that would serve to deceive and cheat one person out of what is fairly due them in order to benefit the one who possesses the faulty weight. In short, it is a crafty and official-looking way to steal from your fellow man. The connection to the sins of Sodom would be that those who do not care for the poor and needy would be inclined to take advantage of their deprived situation. This is, perhaps, one of the abominations committed by the men of Sodom that so provoked the Creator to remove them.

So far in this inventory of offenses, we have not seen the one thing that most associate with Sodom. How interesting! In fact, we could say that the sins listed so far are descriptive of many people and even nations, particularly the United States. America is full of pride and full of food; Americans top the scales when it comes to obesity and consequently, diseases related to rich, fattening foods. Also, we are afflicted with an abundance of idleness so much so that we invent even more convenient ways to offend the Creator.

It could be said that many Americans, particularly leaders, operate a false balance. If the common man does not pay his taxes, he is faced with liens, seizure of property and sometimes prison. If you know the right people, you might only get a slap on the wrist. If you commit a criminal act and know the right people, you might get a pass and be spared the embarrassment of a trial and conviction. In numerous cases, we see how laws now being passed apply only to those who are not "privileged" enough to hold high office.

Certain labor unions are given special treatment by those in government positions in return for loyalty and support. Consequently, those belonging to these unions might be guaranteed a job at the expense of non-union workers. Mainstream media may or may not decide to report on these kinds of injustices, because they too have an agenda and know who it benefits them to protect or to persecute. All of these are examples of a false balance, and all of these happen every day in America.

Suffice it to say, our culture is strikingly similar to what God described when He indicted the men of Sodom. If similar in behavior, what should we expect in consequence? Furthermore, consider that based on what He cited against them, their sins could be summarized this way: they did NOT love the LORD with all of their heart, and they did NOT love their neighbor as themselves. They were, in a word, selfish, and this self-absorbed inclination is what led them to commit what God called *abomination*. What did He mean by that?

> "You shall not lie with a male as with a woman. It is an abomination."
>
> – LEVITICUS 18:22-23

We suggest that this is the abomination committed by the men of Sodom, but we also suggest that their other sins came first and are what eventually led to this sin. In other words, they likely did not jump to this extreme lifestyle overnight. They weren't born that way; they most likely graduated to that extreme by first giving in to pride, gluttony, laziness and disregard for their fellow man. Or shall we put it this way: they began to slowly turn from Truth and Life and eventually looked upon the other Tree—the one that seemed good but rendered a deadly fruit. In the end, they broke away from anything that resembled truth and life, and as a result:

> "God also gave them up to uncleanness, in the lusts of their hearts, to dishonor their bodies among themselves, who exchanged the truth of God for the lie, and worshiped and served the creature rather than the Creator, who is blessed forever. Amen. For this reason God gave them up to vile passions. For even their women exchanged the natural use for what is against nature. Likewise also the men, leaving the natural use of the woman, burned in their lust for one another, men with men committing what is shameful, and receiving in themselves the penalty of their error which was due."
>
> – ROMANS 1:24-27

According to what Paul said here, we see again that God will give mankind what He wants; He will turn him over to the passions of his heart so that in the end he may discover it was not what he needed. It is oftentimes much too late by the time people come to that realization. Unfortunately, some never do; they belligerently go to their grave in defiance against God, His Word and His provocation to repent.

> "O Lord, are not Your eyes on the truth? You have stricken them, but they have not grieved; You have consumed them, but they have refused to receive correction. They have made their faces harder than rock; they have refused to return."
>
> — JEREMIAH 5:3

> "And men were scorched with great heat, and they blasphemed the name of God who has power over these plagues; and they did not repent and give Him glory ... they gnawed their tongues because of the pain. They blasphemed the God of heaven because of their pains and their sores, and did not repent of their deeds"
>
> — REVELATION 16:9 - 11

It is our conviction that man does not get to the point of complete reprobation overnight. It is a gradual metamorphosis of sorts, but one that is inevitable if pride and wickedness go unchecked. When a society devolves into such unabated rebellion as Sodom, that left to its own devices would spread death to other societies, there is but one answer—destruction.

If America has been guilty of the same transgressions that plagued Sodom—pride, fullness of food, laziness, mistreatment of the poor—can we expect to escape the subsequent fruit of that sin, the abomination of nature itself? If we give ourselves over to this abomination, or at least embrace the passive acceptance of it as normal, can we hope to escape the consequence? Sure, this particular lifestyle has always been with us, but we would argue that never before in American history has it been so prevalent and so aggressive.

You see, it is no longer just small groups in scattered pockets of the country who embrace and promote this behavior. It is now accepted by a majority of Americans and is sanctioned and defended by our government at state and federal levels. We have now come to the place in our history where we have taken it upon ourselves to redefine what law is and what constitutes a covenant. We have proudly and defiantly declared that the union between two members of the same sex is legally and morally equivalent to the union that God ordained in the beginning between a husband and wife. We have officially broken this covenant.

MARRIAGE EQUALITY DOES NOT EQUAL LIFE

One of the first covenants addressed in Scripture, perhaps *the* first covenant, is the one between a man and his wife. From the beginning, it is written:

> "And the LORD God said, 'It is not good that man should be alone; I will make him a helper comparable to him.'... And the LORD God caused a deep sleep to fall on Adam, and he slept; and He took one of his ribs, and closed up the flesh in its place. Then the rib which the LORD God had taken from man He made into a woman, and He brought her to the man. And Adam said, 'This is now bone of my bones, and flesh of my flesh; she shall be called Woman, because she was taken out of Man.' Therefore a man shall leave his father and his mother, and be joined to his wife: and they shall become one flesh."
>
> – GENESIS 2:18, 21-24

The purpose of this union was that they could be "fruitful and multiply" (Gen. 1:28). In fact, He blessed that purpose because it was centered upon propagating life. Notice that in order for this to become a reality, God gave him a wife who was to function as his helper. The Hebrew term for helper is *ezer k'negdo,* which is literally "a helper who is his opposite." Alternative renderings are "a helper like his opposite" or even "help-opposite." There are many ways to look at this and expound upon the woman's purpose in the man's life, but considering our topic, we will remain focused on this point: God did not give the man a help-similar.

In fact, the Scripture makes the point that all creatures on earth were brought before Adam so that he could name them, and it was said that there was not an appropriate mate for him. Consequently, God had to make the appropriate mate, and it wasn't another Adam. That union would not allow for the purpose of marriage, which is to propagate life. So it was that the covenant and law that God established was between husband and wife, male and female. Today we are being swayed by public opinion and the courts to concede that male-and-male or female-and-female unions are just as appropriate and should be deemed equal. Obviously, they are not and never shall be.

Regardless of how much people try to make these "marriages" equal to traditional marriages, they will always come up short. These same-sex couples are allowed to adopt — some introduce artificial insemination or surrogate mothers into the relationship — so that they can have a "family," but NO same-sex relationship will ever be able to produce offspring. No same-sex marriage will ever be able to be "fruitful and multiply." These unions cannot produce life, and if not able to produce life, by default they render death.

It's the same old story as from the beginning, just told a different way. Mankind habitually looks upon the other tree as pleasant to the eye, good for food and desirable to make one wise. Still, despite all our attempts to arrive at a different result, death keeps staring us in the face!

In spite of the biblical prohibition against these relationships and the obvious intent of the Creator for marriage, at the time of this writing, over 30 states plus the District of Columbia allow marriage for same-sex couples. The Federal government has gone to great lengths to defend these unions as being protected by the U.S. Constitution. America has taken it upon herself to second-guess God and, after 6,000 years of historical and legal precedent, redefine His interpretation of marriage. We have perverted His definition of this covenant in order to establish our own amended version. We have anointed the unsanctified as sacred and legalized what God calls an abomination! Considering the following, perhaps we should reconsider:

> "(He) did not spare the ancient world, but saved Noah, one of eight people, a preacher of righteousness, bringing in the flood on the world of the ungodly; and turning the cities of Sodom and Gomorrah into ashes, condemned them to destruction, making them an example to those who afterward would live ungodly."
>
> — 2 Peter 2:5-6

"As Sodom and Gomorrah, and the cities around them in a similar manner to these, having given themselves over to sexual immorality and gone after strange flesh, are set forth as an example, suffering the vengeance of eternal fire. Likewise also these dreamers defile the flesh, reject authority, and speak evil of dignitaries."

– JUDE 1:7-8

To speak of such consequences in this day and time is regarded as bigoted, racist and hateful by those who have determined that their pursuits are just as normal and acceptable as those who follow a traditional path. No matter—neither their opinions nor their lawsuits can unseat the truth. We can wish all we want for clouds to be made from cotton candy, but it won't change reality.

When we make lawful what God said is unlawful, we invite the repercussions. When we call blessed what He has cursed, we have not removed the curse but have invited it upon our heads. Politicians and political pundits may do their utmost to sway public opinion in favor of such behavior, but the Almighty will not be moved!

Considering that we are living in times likened unto the days of Noah, is it a mere coincidence, or perhaps ironic, that the LGBT community have adopted the rainbow as their banner? Oddly enough, the rainbow is a sign of the covenant God made with every living creature in the day that Noah departed from the ark (Gen. 9:13-17).

"And I will remember my covenant, which is between me and you and every living creature of all flesh; and the waters shall never again become a flood to destroy all flesh."

– GENESIS 9:15

Considering that Sodom's primary sin was determined by the Creator to be pride, is it coincidental that the LGBT community sponsors Gay Pride marches across America? These marches are intended to raise awareness of their belief that gays, lesbians and transgender people are just as natural and ordinary as the everyday heterosexual. It is very troubling and even dangerous that more and more Americans are willing to accept that view.

With America following the pattern of Sodom—repeating their sins and following their example—should we not also expect the same outcome? While God did promise to never again destroy the earth with a flood of waters, He did not promise to never again destroy a community with fire. If we continue to mock God in this manner, are our cities doomed to burn?

GOD AND GAYS

We should interject here that the God we serve does not long to destroy people; no, He longs to restore people. Peter wrote:

> "The Lord is not slack concerning His promise, as some count slackness, but is longsuffering toward us, not willing that any should perish but that all should come to repentance."
>
> – 2 PETER 3:9

Peter makes mention of God's longsuffering in his first epistle as well, noting that the entire time the ark was being built by Noah, God was withholding judgment to allow for as many people as would to come to repentance. Again, God does not wish for people to be destroyed but that all would come to repentance. So we can conclude that God loves the person who chooses a gay lifestyle, but He calls this lifestyle unnatural and an abomination. God loves the person who chooses to become a thief or robber; however, He still commands, "You shall not steal."

You get the picture: God loves everyone. We are told, "For God so loved the world that He gave His only Son that whosoever should believe on Him should not perish but have everlasting life," but does that mean it is right for churches and ministers to say it is okay to be gay and that God approves of them as they are? Speaking for Himself, the Creator said:

> The Lord, the Lord God, merciful and gracious, longsuffering, and abounding in goodness and truth, keeping mercy for thousands, forgiving iniquity and transgression and sin, by no means clearing the guilty, visiting the iniquity of the fathers upon the

children and the children's children to the third and the fourth
generation."

— EXODUS 34:6-7

"Therefore know that the Lord your God, He is God, the faithful
God who keeps covenant and mercy for a thousand generations
with those who love Him and keep His commandments; and He
repays those who hate Him to their face, to destroy them. He
will not be slack with him who hates Him; He will repay him
to his face."

— DEUTERONOMY 7:9-10

When comparing these passages, something about our Heavenly
Father becomes perfectly clear: He is far more merciful and willing
to forgive than He is ready to bring judgment upon the guilty. If we
were to put the number of generations that will be punished (3-4) in
one tray on the Scale of Justice and the number of generations that are
shown mercy (1000) in the other, the scale would tilt toward mercy
very quickly. That is how we are to perceive our Father—merciful.

However, we cannot neglect the fact that the guilty and unrepentant will be punished. Also, His mercy is promised *only* to those who
love Him and who keep His commandments. No such guarantee is
given to those who don't love Him and who don't abide by His Word.
Even though the Scale of Justice is tipped overwhelmingly toward
mercy, each time we sin—whether individually or nationally—we
put another weight onto the tray of judgment. Sooner or later it will
counter the weights on the tray of mercy and tip in the other direction.

Mercy was extended to the Amorites in the days of Abraham
because the "iniquity of the Amorites" was not yet full (Gen. 15:16).
But when Joshua and the children of Israel arrived 400 years later, they
were told to wipe out the inhabitants of the land because apparently
their time to repent had expired. Likewise, if our cup of iniquity continues to fill and eventually overflows, then mercy will be outweighed
by justice and God will certainly act. While we appeal to His compassion and mercy, we cannot afford to ignore the fact that when the scale
tilts in the other direction, judgment will be poured out.

So, whether the issue is gay marriage, abortion or a number of other contentious issues, is culture justified in redefining laws and covenants that were first ordained by God just because we live in the 21st century? Will politicians and political activists be exempt from judgment just because they were responding to the wants and desires of their constituencies? Is it appropriate for churches, synagogues and ministers to concede to the whims of society just because it is politically and economically expedient? Not likely!

As a matter of fact, the list of transgressions recorded in Ezekiel 16 was not so much an indictment of Sodom as it was an indictment of Jerusalem and the people of Judah. Putting everything into context, it is clear that God cited the gross misconduct that led to Sodom's destruction in order to show that the sins of His people exceeded that of "your sister, Sodom."

> "Your elder sister is Samaria, who dwells with her daughters to the north of you; and your younger sister, who dwells to the south of you, is Sodom and her daughters. You did not walk in their ways nor act according to their abominations; but, as if that were too little, you became more corrupt than they in all your ways. As I live, says the Lord God, neither your sister Sodom nor her daughters have done as you and your daughters have done."
>
> – EZEKIEL 16:46-48

Our point is this: it is one thing for culture to engage in sins and debauchery, but it is another matter entirely for God's people to accommodate or embrace those deeds. When we let our guard down in this respect, those thoughts, ideas and philosophies will eventually creep into God's house and corrupt His people, just as certainly as the world is corrupt.

Case and point: today there are Christian publications advocating for and distributing the message that God is okay with the gay and lesbian lifestyle and even with same-sex marriage. More and more believers are buying into this notion. Yet, Scripture is clear on the matter; this lifestyle renders death, and to endorse it invites judgment.

Count the Costs

In the book of Judges, it is recorded that a Levite and his concubine were journeying from Bethlehem and happened to come into Gibeah, a village inhabited by those of the tribe of Benjamin. Because it was late in the day and no one would take him into their house, he and his party remained in the public square until an elderly man happened upon them. He invited them to spend the night in his house with the promise of provision and the warning not to remain in the village square.

> "As they were enjoying themselves, suddenly certain men of the city, perverted men (literally, *sons of Belial*) surrounded the house and beat on the door. They spoke to the master of the house, the old man, saying, 'Bring out the man who came to your house, that we may know him carnally!'"
>
> – JUDGES 19:22

This sounds amazingly similar to the episode in Sodom on the night before its destruction when the perverted men of the city came looking to defile two angels they mistook to be men. As in the story of Lot, the old man refused to release him to them and offered instead his own virgin daughter and the man's concubine. Eventually, the concubine was turned over to them and by sunrise was laying just outside the door, dead.

There are two components to this story that need to be considered; first, there is the aggressive and violent nature of the men who ravaged and murdered a helpless victim. Then there are the ones who accommodated their violence and perversion. Frankly, it's hard to say which sin was worse—the act of commission or the one of omission. Nonetheless, death was the result.

As the story continues, 400 thousand men of war from the other tribes of Israel were so shocked by the brutality of these Benjaminites that they determined to go and destroy the men who did this. When they arrived at Gibeah and demanded the surrender of the guilty parties, the people of Gibeah refused and enlisted the aid of other

Benjaminites. When all was said and done, over 25,000 men of Benjamin were killed, decimating the tribe to the point that the other tribes of Israel feared this twelfth tribe would be no more.

Here is the point: Although Benjamin did continue as a tribe, they almost became extinct because a violent and aggressive spirit was granted safe quarter among them. Of all of the Benjaminites who fell by the sword, very few, if any, were directly involved with what happened to the Levite's concubine. However, the entire tribe was guilty because they harbored such corruption within their borders. In other words, those who accommodated the sin were just as guilty as those who committed the act.

What is at stake when God's people bow to the pressures of society and decide to co-exist with and accommodate that which God disdains? Consider Lot: he is an excellent reminder of what it costs us when we choose unwisely. He reminds us of what is at stake when we are in the wrong place at the wrong time. Lot and his family provide the most heart-rending example of what can happen to our families if we choose to align ourselves with the wrong crowd, regardless of what the short-term benefits might appear to be.

How is it that Lot ended up in Sodom in the first place? According to Scripture, he saw something that looked good from a distance, but he obviously did not notice the inherent wickedness that had taken up residence there. Consequently, Lot and his entire family lived among some of the most ungodly and violent people who ever lived. The greatest tragedy of his choice, however, was that he lost influence over most of his loved ones, most of whom chose to stay even as God prepared to destroy the place. Even among those who did flee, his companion for life never really left—she looked back and perished. Lot's choice to co-exist with the Sodomites cost him dearly.

Sadly, some of God's people are making the same unwise and unsafe choice today. Perhaps it is because of political expediency, fear of losing their tax-exempt status or maybe because they have convinced themselves that God is really okay with this lifestyle. Some have chosen to accommodate it, endorse it and co-exist with it. God help us, because when Israel allowed for the uninhibited exercise of this lifestyle, it was devastating!

> "And there were also sodomites in the land: and they did according to all the abominations of the nations which the LORD cast out before the children of Israel. And it came to pass in the fifth year of king Rehoboam, that Shishak king of Egypt came up against Jerusalem: and he took away the treasures of the house of the LORD, and the treasures of the king's house; he even took away all: and he took away all the shields of gold which Solomon had made."
>
> – 1 KINGS 14:24-26 (KJV)

Our discussion of these harsh realities is not to demean, castigate or alienate anyone, because as we mentioned earlier, God desires not to destroy anyone but to restore everyone. However, there are some things that illicit His response, especially when dealing with a people who have entered into covenant with Him. When He responds to wickedness by removing His Spirit, another aggressive and destructive spirit will most certainly move in, bringing with it conflict, chaos, violence and ruin. To some degree, the spirit of liberty has already been usurped by another spirit. This spirit professes liberty and equality but is antagonistic toward God and the laws of nature that He ordained. This particular spirit is not the only one plaguing the land, but it is the one that has taken center stage in the political and national spotlight.

As approval ratings begin to turn in favor of issues such as same-sex marriage, it is becoming evident that our collective way of thinking is changing and that our country is undergoing a massive and detrimental transformation. Also, considering the issues we have highlighted here, the evidence seems to say that God is lifting His Hand and with that motion is also lifting the hedge. If we truly are losing the cover of His protective wing, then America will eventually be dethroned as the world's superpower, and another power will rise in its place. If we have failed to guard what was entrusted to us, then there is bound to be a changing of the guard!

CHAPTER TEN

Fade To Black

*"Thus he said, 'The fourth beast shall be the fourth
kingdom upon earth, which shall be diverse from all
kingdoms, and shall devour the whole earth, and shall
tread it down, and break it in pieces. And the ten horns
out of this kingdom are ten kings that shall arise.'"*

– DANIEL 7:23-24

A s WE SAID in beginning of this book, the heart and essence of
the covenant with God is to love Him with all of our heart
and to love our neighbor as ourselves. Consequently, when
people enter into a covenant with Him, they also commit themselves
to being in covenant with one another. The covenantal relationship is
not just between a person and God, but between that person, God,
and their fellow man. This was the call to Israel, and it is our call as
well.

What we do and how we live is not exclusively for our benefit but so
that, like Abraham, we might be a source of blessing to others. We are
called to this mission, not because we are special, but that we might
serve a special purpose—to be a light to others. When Israel failed to
do this, nations of the world had no light to guide them, did not hold
Israel in high esteem and were typically given opportunity to harass
Israel. As the Body of Messiah, when we fail to be that light and to

uphold the covenant, not only to do we suffer, but others suffer as well, having no true light to guide them.

Based on this principle, if America was called to be a beacon of liberty and righteousness founded upon Godly principles and committed to a covenant with the Almighty, yet we walk away from that, we will suffer the consequences just as we have expounded throughout this book. Other nations, the helpless and the weak throughout the world, will suffer the consequences of our failure as well. Our decline will provide those with not-so-noble aspirations the opportunity to rise up and take our place.

Perhaps those nations and leaders who already smell blood are even now positioning themselves to expand their power and influence over their weaker neighbors. We are definitely seeing this kind of aggression on the part of Putin in Russia. There is increased saber rattling coming from the North Koreans, and most bothersome are the very troubling developments in the Middle East and the sudden rise of ISIS.

SUNSET IN THE WEST, MOONRISE IN THE EAST

In spite of a decade-long war against fanatical Islam, are we seeing its demise or its resurgence? If you were to ask the politicians, you would get varying responses depending on their own agendas. Given the news accounts of multiple beheadings, seizure of assets and desert strongholds, it would seem there is a resurgence of fanaticism and renewed fervor to implement fundamental Islamic control over the entire Middle Eastern region. In the likes of ISIS (the Islamic State of Iraq and Syria also known as IS, the Islamic State), many believe we are witnessing the emergence of an Islamic caliphate, an entity that would impose the harsh will of *sharia* (Islamic law) upon all who find themselves trapped within its clutches.

For months, multiple reports coming from the besieged territories in the Levant confirm that these murderous thugs compel those not of their particular strain of Islam to convert, pay tribute, leave with nothing, or die. Tens-of-thousands are suffering under their heel. Aside from the vicious slaughter of so many innocent people in the

East, perhaps the greatest insult being imposed on the West by this group is that their success is due largely to the windfall of arms and equipment provided for them indirectly by the American taxpayer. This was made possible by the decision to withdraw U.S. troops from Iraq against the advice of most military and congressional advisers.

Political pundits and military strategists are warning that this is a very dangerous situation, not only for those directly in their path but eventually for those of us in the West and particularly the United States. The President has been strongly encouraged to take military action against ISIS—and to some degree he has—because it is feared that if we do not, the black banner of ISIS will be seen in American cities and towns.

Indeed, several threats have been made against the U.S. by their leader and by members of their ranks, including a vow to fly their flag — a banner that proclaims, "There is no God but Allah and Muhammad is his messenger" — over the White House. Are these to be considered idle threats or something to be taken seriously? Given the fact that the White House has already proven to be somewhat vulnerable recently, can we really afford to disregard the threat from ISIS?

Seeing that there is this sudden shift of power in the East, essentially erasing whatever gains the U.S. and the West may have accomplished in the Iraq War, it would strongly suggest that ISIS, Hamas, Hezbollah and the like sense that now is the time to act. Why? There is an obvious lack of respect on their part for the ability and the will of the United States to act in any way that would impede their aggression.

Many in the East—and this would likely include Putin of Russia—sense that the United States has weak leadership. They sense that America is on the decline and may be on the verge of such internal strife and crisis that it would be incapable of mounting any serious response to ISIS, Iran, North Korea, or Russia should any of these, or all combined—God forbid—mount any military action against their neighbors. If this proves to be true, then the stage is set for events we've heard about all our lives to unfold.

Eschatologists have long pondered what must happen to America whereby Gog of Magog feels at liberty to invade Israel and why there is no one, save God, to come to her defense. As we have contemplated this over the years, the only conclusion that seems plausible is that America doesn't respond because she either can't or won't. Either situation infers a dramatic decline in America's influence, power and most importantly her spiritual well-being. The tragic developments in the Middle East, beginning with the so-called Arab Spring right up to the emergence of ISIS, are directly related to what is going on in the United States. Wildfire is being ignited in the Middle East because the lamp of liberty in the West is being reduced to smoldering embers.

With that in mind, let us go back to something we discussed earlier in the book—the 2011 demonstrations of the so-called 99%. As we related to you, this mob (and that is what it was) staged occupation after occupation, which included public defecation, sex acts, and even sexual assaults, all across the nation claiming throughout the protests a political and ethical kinship with their "brothers in Egypt." By that they meant their protests were an attempt to replicate the intent and methods of the so-called "Arab Spring." You may recall that the Arab Spring was about revolution and toppling those in power and was often accompanied by mob violence, including murder and rape!

Considering that identifying with their Arab brothers was the intention of the Occupy Wall Street crowd, (some of whom moved on to other hotspots such as Ferguson, Missouri), let us briefly focus on the word *arab* or, in Hebrew, *arav*. The word actually means "mixed, mingled," and is used to describe the "mixed multitude"—the *arav rav*, those who incited Israel to complain and rebel in the wilderness. Would this concept not define those who call themselves the 99%? Might this also explain why, on the campuses of some American universities, there are protests against Israel, the desecration of the American flag and rallies in support of ISIS and Hamas?

As we pointed out earlier, Americans need to realize that our enemies are not always external ones. True, there are many enemies abroad, but unfortunately America has many enemies within who claim to identify with other revolutionaries, Marxists, Communists, and as in this case, the same strain of people who are murdering countless victims in the name of Allah.

Recent reports suggest that thousands of Muslims and many Islamic converts, including some from the U.S., are pouring into Syria and Iraq to join ISIS in their effort to establish a caliphate. Any way you look at it, whether abroad or at home, there is an emerging power — another spirit — that is fundamentally opposed to what traditional America, the America that was founded upon biblical principles, is all about. As the United States splinters, our adversaries are coming together for a common purpose — to bring America down. This ascending power is fundamentally opposed to the God of Israel, His Word and His people and desires to destroy them all. In a word, it is Antichrist!

THE PEOPLE OF THE EAST

> "And the sixth angel poured out his vial upon the great river Euphrates; and the water thereof was dried up, that the way of the kings of the east might be prepared."
>
> — REVELATION 16:12

According to Scripture, there will be significant political and religious coalitions forming in the last days in order to provoke revolution and war and to expand their influence. They will most likely be looking to fill the position of dominant power that will presumably be vacated by the United States. These coalitions include what John called the "kings from the East," an army of 200 million men that many suppose will be comprised of the Chinese and perhaps North Koreans.

Actually, there is adequate reason to believe that these kings from the East are Islamic forces because in the Scriptures on multiple occasions, the Ishmaelites, Amalekites and Midianites — nations all hailing from modern Arab territories — are referred to as "the people of the east." One such example involves those who came against Israel in the days of Gideon.

> "Then the children of Israel did evil in the sight of the Lord. So the Lord delivered them into the hand of Midian for seven years, and the hand of Midian prevailed against Israel. Because of the Midianites, the children of Israel made for themselves the dens, the caves, and the strongholds which are in the mountains. So it was, whenever Israel had sown, Midianites would come up; also

Amalekites and the people of the East would come up against them."

– JUDGES 6:1-3

There are several points of interest in these verses beginning with the fact that the "people of the east" were able to harass and overpower God's people because Israel did "evil in the sight of the LORD." This is more evidence that when God's people abandon the covenant, God hides His face, allowing another presence to move in and lord over His people. Furthermore, this Arab coalition oppressed Israel for seven years, devouring their crops and stealing their livelihood. Interestingly, later in the story we read that the people of the east are likened to locusts, an insect infamous for devouring anything green and fruitful.

"Now the Midianites and Amalekites, all the people of the East, were lying in the valley as numerous as locusts; and their camels were without number."

– JUDGES 7:12

The "people of the east" being likened unto locusts is fascinating for several reasons. Chief among them is the fact that, from the beginning to the end of Scripture, locusts are depicted as "armies" sent to quickly overcome and desolate a nation. For instance, locusts descended upon Egypt and devoured every green thing in the land.

"So Moses stretched out his rod over the land of Egypt, and the Lord brought an east wind on the land all that day and all that night. When it was morning, the east wind brought the locusts. And the locusts went up over all the land of Egypt and rested on all the territory of Egypt. They were very severe; previously there had been no such locusts as they, nor shall there be such after them. For they covered the face of the whole earth, so that the land was darkened; and they ate every herb of the land and all the fruit of the trees which the hail had left. So there remained nothing green on the trees or on the plants of the field throughout all the land of Egypt."

– EXODUS 10:13-15

Notice what God used to bring in this vast swarm of locusts— "an east wind." That is understood to be, from Egypt's perspective, a wind that comes from the east moving westward. Considering that the eastern border of Egypt is mostly shoreline along the Red Sea, it means this wind came from the direction of what we now call Saudi Arabia. We could say that the "east wind" was an "Arabian wind." This is what ushered in the locusts that helped to destroy the nation of Egypt. By the way, while there is no mention of locusts in the story, it was an "east wind" that scorched the seven withered ears of grain in Joseph's dream, an event that initiated a seven-year famine (Gen. 41:23). This would further suggest that the "east wind"—synonymous with locusts and the people of the east—is something that brings destruction upon a nation.

Other passages link locusts and the people of the east with desolation, such as in the book of Joel. In chapter one of his prophecy, he describes four different types of locusts as coming against the land of Israel, devouring everything in sight. If one type of locust leaves something, the next wave will eat it, and so on, until all four have gone through the land leaving nothing. In the second chapter, Joel describes the scene this way.

> "Let all the inhabitants of the land tremble; for the day of the Lord is coming, for it is at hand: A day of darkness and gloominess, a day of clouds and thick darkness, like the morning clouds spread over the mountains. A people come, great and strong, the like of whom has never been; nor will there ever be any such after them, even for many successive generations. A fire devours before them, and behind them a flame burns; the land is like the Garden of Eden before them, and behind them a desolate wilderness; surely nothing shall escape them."
>
> – JOEL 2:1-3

This passage is describing locusts. As they approach "the land" (which is the land of Israel), it is likened to the Garden of Eden. Behind them, in the direction from which they are coming, is a wilderness. In other words, these locusts come into the land from an eastern wilderness. East of Israel and toward Iraq and Saudi Arabia is a vast and desolate wilderness. It is the same area that is seeing an incredible amount of distressing news presently.

We can couple this information with a passage from Revelation 9 describing locust-like creatures that harass and sting men for five months and whose "king" is called Abaddon or Destroyer (Rev. 9:1-11). When you consider all of these verses collectively, it seems very possible that there is a connection between the "people of the east" and Revelation's "kings from the east." If there is still any doubt about this connection, then consider what happens at the conclusion of the battle between Gideon's 300 and the people of the east.

> "So Gideon arose and killed Zebah and Zalmunna, and took the *crescent* ornaments that were on their camels' necks."
>
> – JUDGES 8:21

It seems impossible that what we understand from the past regarding the "people of the east" and what we see happening today in the Middle East could be considered a mere coincidence. To the contrary, what we are witnessing may represent the embryonic stages in the formation of a coalition that Scripture calls "the kings from the east" and a ten-nation confederacy described by Daniel in his prophecy and by John in the book of Revelation, known as the "ten kings."

Certainly there are other coalitions being formed throughout the world, and we would agree that they all play some role in the overall scheme of things in the last days. However, at the epicenter of everything regarding the last days is God's people and the nation of Israel. Though many of these political coalitions are not a friend to Israel, none is more violent or dangerous than this future Islamic confederacy. When this coalition becomes a reality, it will be presided over by none other than the Antichrist, a person who seeks to steal, kill and destroy anything and anyone associated with the God of Abraham, Isaac and Jacob.

RESURRECTING THE CALIPHATE

Without being too exhaustive, let's review a few things the Bible tells us about the Beast and the kingdom of the Antichrist. To begin with, according to all biblical accounts it is an incredibly violent kingdom. Daniel describes it as being terrifying, dreadful and having "iron teeth" with which it devours and breaks everything it encounters. Should anything escape its teeth, it uses its feet to stamp on and destroy it (Dan. 7:7). According to John, it will violently overthrow nations, and no one will be able stop it or prevail against it (Rev. 13:4). Furthermore, its people will behead anyone who follows any other faith, particularly those who believe in and follow Christ (Rev. 20:4).

There are other facets we could examine regarding the Beast, but what we have just mentioned about this murderous kingdom is enough to convince us that what Daniel and John described is exactly what we are witnessing in the Middle East today. In other words, there is no doubt in our minds that the kingdom of the Beast is Islamic and may be taking shape right now and right where it is supposed to—in the heart of ancient Babylon. Understanding that the beginning tells the end (Isa. 46:10), the first great empire was Babylon and it was ruled by a rebel and tyrant—first Nimrod and then Nebuchadnezzar. It only makes sense that in the end, the last empire will also arise in ancient Babylon and will be ruled by a rebel and tyrant—you won't find Rome in the beginning.

The reality of the situation is this: while many still look for a united European and Roman beast system to take shape in the West, radical Islam is on the move in the East. Every year, as many as ten-thousand Christians are martyred at the hands of Muslims in places like Nigeria, Kenya, Syria, Egypt, Iran and now Iraq. Many are tortured before they are murdered. Some are crucified or beheaded. Complicating the issue is the fact that two-thirds of the world's Christians currently live in what should be regarded as dangerous areas, many of them in the path of Islamic radicals such as ISIS.

The stated goal of ISIS—a group so vicious that even Al Qaeda wanted nothing to do with them—is to resurrect a Sunni-led Islamic caliphate. This would be devastating to anyone who objects to their beliefs, especially Christians who live within the domain of the caliphate. As we've already witnessed in areas controlled by ISIS, *sharia* would be imposed upon the lands that they dominate, effectively unseating age-old customs and laws that have existed in these places. This is interesting because, according to Daniel, this is exactly one of the things the Beast is expected to do.

> "He shall speak pompous words against the Most High, shall persecute the saints of the Most High, and shall intend to change times and law."
>
> – DANIEL 7:25

One of the first things people unaccustomed to *sharia* would notice would be that a ban would be placed on all other faiths and their respective days of worship, including holidays. Friday—the sixth day—would be considered the day of worship. Only holidays associated with Islam would be allowed. Those accustomed to the Gregorian calendar would have no choice but to adjust to the Islamic calendar, which is based on the sighting of the new moon and contains 354 days. In short, *sharia* would forcefully change your way of life.

Calendar changes would be the least of worries though. Right now, in parts of Syria and Iraq, a person who does not know how to properly answer an ISIS inquisitor in matters of the Quran or who tries to sneak to their church to worship, may end up in a ditch or on the side of the road with a bullet in their head—or worse, with their head on a pike in the village square!

That is how the "peaceful" religion of Islam is imposed on those unfortunate enough to fall under its control. Additionally, those who hope to remain in their homes must be able to pay a very stiff tax—regarded as tribute or ransom—arbitrarily imposed each year by those in power. If they cannot pay the tax, they are forced to leave their home or die.

Another attribute of the caliphate is that it is ruled by one man, the Caliph, even though it is considered an Islamic state comprised of many nations. That means anyone who lives within the caliphate would be subject to the rule and whims of one man; no representative form of government, no elections (none that have any real meaning, anyway) and no dissenting views would be tolerated. His word would be law because Islam believes that this man has been granted supreme authority by Allah. This scenario sounds like an ideal match for the one the Bible calls the Antichrist; in Islam he is called *al Mahdi*.

BLACK BANNERS RISING

There is a tradition among many Sunnis in Syria and Iraq that when *al Mahdi* arrives, the people must submit to him because Allah has sent him to establish a universal government of peace and prosperity. However, peace will come only after a terrible war. Interestingly enough, these are the very places beset with war and where ISIS is attempting to unseat sitting governments and dissolve the borders between the two nations in order to create one Islamic state.

Since the beginning of the Arab Spring, Syria has been engulfed in a fierce civil war that has claimed the lives of over 140,000 people—many of them innocent victims. As people continue to die, some are starting to earnestly consider the words of the *hadiths* (Islamic traditions) and answer the call to arms being issued by the jihadists of ISIS. These traditions are very interesting in light of current events because in some cases they seem to suggest that ISIS and its leader, Abu Bakr al-Baghdadi, may be heralding the rise of the caliphate and the arrival of *al Mahdi*.

It is alleged that Mohammad foretold of black banners coming from the east and that the Islamic warriors who fight for this banner will have hearts "as firm as iron." This army, comprised of "mighty men with long hair and beards" (*haddith Asmel Masalik*), is the one that is supposed to subdue many lands and, eventually, march successfully into Jerusalem under the leadership of *al Mahdi,* who, according to their tradition, is followed by none other than Jesus.

We cannot be certain that ISIS is the fulfillment of biblical prophecy concerning the rise of the Beast. For that matter, we cannot be certain that ISIS will fulfill Islamic expectations concerning the "coming enlightened one"—*al Mahdi*. We can be certain that these are very violent men and very committed Muslims who believe that this is the hour to resurrect the Islamic caliphate and subdue anyone who gets in their way. That they have chosen to establish this Islamic state in the very place where the Bible foretold that the Beast would rise—in the heart of ancient Babylonia—cannot be happenstance.

Considering these points and the obvious zeal of ISIS to conquer, kill and behead helpless victims and to advertise it to the world, we can certainly say it is unlike anything we have ever seen. The level of commitment is frightening when you consider that ISIS seized control of a chemical weapons storage facility at the Al-Muthanna complex in which was stored tons of saran gas. These weapon stores were left over from the Saddam Hussein era and classified as useless but too dangerous to move. Whatever the status, the fact is ISIS now has control of it.

Though we know that one day Babylon will be resurrected and the Beast will rise from among the nations (Rev. 13:1-4), we cannot be completely certain of what will become of this present situation where ISIS is concerned. There are other issues brewing in the same region in places like Iran and Gaza that merit concern. There are the issues between Russia and some of her former Soviet-era states and satellites. There is the economic threat that China poses. We could go on and on.

The point of raising the issue of ISIS is to point out what *can* and *will* happen when a people—a nation—raised up by God to be a light allows that light to flicker and go out. As we stated in the very beginning, it is less likely for a tyrant to rise in the East if the West is strong, resolute and righteous. Regrettably, that is not the case at present. Just as the hard-heartedness of Pharaoh and his counselors subjected the land of Egypt to sorrow and destruction, so we too, a wayward nation resistant to God's reproof, await the consequences.

We fear the locusts may already be coming, riding upon an east wind, to cover the land with darkness and desolation. And as liberty's light slowly smothers under their weight, glorious shades of red, white and blue fade to black.

AFTERWORD

As for Me and My House

"In those days there was no king in Israel;
everyone did what was right in his own eyes."

– JUDGES 21:25

THE ABOVE STATEMENT is the essence of the problem that has stricken God's people from the very beginning—doing what is right in their own eyes. Never has that approach worked well for any of God's people. It has always led to disappointment, destruction and death.

This statement also summarizes the state of affairs in America today. Scores of kids do whatever is right in their own eyes because their parents don't pay attention or don't have the moral fortitude to do anything about it. People on the street do whatever seems right in their eyes without consideration for how it may affect the person next to them because in today's world many simply could not care less. We could argue that these kinds of things happen in Hometown, USA because our leaders do the same thing in our halls of government.

Today's typical politicians are so fearful of losing an election that they cease to lead as they were elected to do. Instead they follow the whims of the people who, as we just said, tend to do what is right in their own eyes. Political correctness has so infected most everyone in public service that they won't speak the truth but will heartily defend a lie. They certainly won't defend an innocent child in its mother's womb but will cut off the water supply to millions of people, as in California's San Joaquin Valley, in order to protect a non-indigenous 3" fish in San Francisco Bay. When Congress won't do what the President and his administration wants them to do, the Chief Executive will just grab his pen, sign an Executive Order and do what is right in his own eyes — law or no law.

What does all of this mean for America? Obviously, it means that the nation is in deep trouble. Beyond that it means the world is in deep trouble. Remember, the covenant with God encompasses a responsibility to God — keeping His commandments — with the reward being blessing and prosperity. However, there is also the responsibility to our fellow man — the nations of the earth.

God's covenant people — Abraham's seed — were and still are called to be a source of blessing to the entire earth. Likewise, if America has been in covenant with God and has benefited by inheriting unparalleled blessing and prosperity, it has been so that we could share the blessings and prosperity, and more importantly their source, with the nations of the world. But now having broken that covenant because of selfishness, we have not only failed to love and honor God as we should, we have failed to consider our fellowman.

You see, it was never all about the greatness of the United States. It was about the greatness of God's purpose for the United States. Our failure as a nation not only affects us but those we were to aid and support as well. Because America is on the decline, others from every continent on earth will suffer the ramifications in some way small or great. Maybe one of those ramifications of our decline is that those in covenant with another god — a crescent-moon god, perhaps — are on the ascent.

When it comes time to affix blame on the responsible parties, it is typical to point the finger at the other guy. Yet, the fault does not lie with an agnostic teacher, a secular city council or a depraved rock star. The fault lies with us — *His people*. Many years ago, we hearkened unto the voices of those who would reinvent history and have us believe that the Creator and His Word had nothing to do with the founding and development of this nation.

We listened to those clergy who said certain principles in Scripture were archaic and were relevant only when they supported the current culture's ideology and worldview. We embraced a philosophy at war with what the Founders advocated and what the Father has ordained. Somewhere along the way, we forgot that we were established as a "nation under God."

In acknowledgment of our desperate situation, where does all this troubling information leave us? What are we to do? Should we move to a remote location and shift into survival mode? Should we just sit aside and watch our beloved country die? What are we to think? Maybe America is just another empire, one of many that rose to greatness only to fall into oblivion when its purpose has been served.

Maybe like so many great empires before us, we focused so hard on standing strong against our external foes that we forgot to pay attention to the enemy within. When the previous empires grew weak from the disease and corruption within, their enemies abroad had only to apply the right amount of pressure in the proper place to bring them down. Is that where America now finds herself? Are we on the verge of bloodshed and violence? Are we witnessing the final moments of America as we knew it? If that be the case, what do we do?

The answer is "Repent!" As never before, His people need to hear what He is saying through the turmoil and hubbub—"Return to Me and focus on My Kingdom!" Because, as despairing as the world's situation is, we should take heart and remember that He—the LORD God Almighty—really is IN CONTROL, and His Kingdom is forever! Even when the Adversary is permitted to pursue his own agenda—whether against Job long ago or against America today—he always ends up serving our Father's purpose.

In that vein we can confidently conclude based on what the Scripture shares, that our Father's purpose does not call for the United States to be the eternal superpower. Yet, He does call upon His people to be equipped, prepared and ready to play our role in His plan for this time. Understanding that the above statement might be hard for some to swallow, nevertheless, we have to face the fact that we are here to advance the only true superpower—the Kingdom of Heaven—period.

We must keep in mind that for this to happen, it will eventually require that every kingdom of man, including America, take a back seat to God's Kingdom. Therefore, as a believer we must be careful not to get caught up in a temporal point of view trying to hold on to something that is destined to become the "kingdoms of our God and of His Christ." Remember, there came a time that even Jerusalem had to answer for her transgressions.

> "When you see Jerusalem surrounded by armies, then know that its desolation is near. Then let those who are in Judea flee to the mountains, let those who are in the midst of her depart, and let not those who are in the country enter her. For these are the days of vengeance, that all things which are written may be fulfilled."
>
> – LUKE 21:20-22

Jesus warned those Judeans who would listen that even a city, a nation, or people that God had chosen for a special purpose are not exempt from punishment if they continue to rebel and break His covenant. Likewise, as much as we love our country and grieve over the things happening to it, we must focus on God's purposes and His Kingdom and stand only on those truths that can withstand the weight of His justice—those are the things that will last. So then, let us set our face upon Him and turn our ear to heed His voice that we might be numbered among those who overcome.

Where ISIS and other such groups are concerned, if they are to be silenced and defeated, ultimately it will not be with bullets and bombs. It will be because God's people here and abroad *repent*. If the Freedom from Religion Foundation and other Godless, progressive organizations are to fail in their attempt to silence God's people, it will be because His people humble themselves and *repent*.

If it is His will that America should return to her former glory, power and influence and be the "shining city on a hill," it will not be determined by who sits in the White House and who does not. It will not be determined by how many conservative justices are appointed to the bench or by how many G-rated movies are produced in Hollywood. If it happens, it will be because "we the people," His people, those called by His name:

> "...humble themselves, and pray and seek my face, and turn from their wicked ways, then I will hear from heaven, and will forgive their sin and HEAL THEIR LAND."
>
> – 2 CHRONICLES 7:14

Rest assured, God is faithful to His promise, and He keeps His covenant with His people. The only question that hangs in the air unanswered is in regard to the covenant and our promise to Him—"Will we keep it?" Will we be faithful to Him regardless of what everyone else does? Realizing that the following statement will not sit well with some, nevertheless, we must say it. The greater issue is not whether the United States, as we have known it, survives. The more relevant issue at hand is whether God's people in America and throughout the globe will turn from their sins, rise up and fulfill the call to be His people.

Will we be faithful to the covenant He has made with us and proclaim His Kingdom and His Righteousness in the face of political correctness? Will we stand for His truth even when it disagrees with the popular notion of tolerance and co-existence? Will we bravely raise the banner of the crucified and risen Messiah even if we come face to face with the black banner of ISIS and the sword of Islam?

We, the people of Messiah—His Body in the earth—are the nation that is to be salt and light, that city set upon a hill that cannot be hidden. It is the responsibility of God's people—the elect—to fill the vacuum of darkness and be the light to all nations by reflecting His light regardless of what others may do. We can no longer afford to follow the trend of society and do what is right in our own eyes. We must choose to do what is right in our Father's eyes. Thus we close with a discourse that was delivered to another generation of God's people but whose words are just as relevant to us today.

> "And if it seems evil to you to serve the Lord, choose for yourselves this day whom you will serve, whether the gods which

your fathers served that were on the other side of the River, or the gods of the Amorites, in whose land you dwell. But as for me and my house, we will serve the Lord."

– JOSHUA 24:15

Amen.

About the Authors

Perry Stone

Evangelist Perry Stone Jr. is founder and president of Voice of Evangelism Outreach Ministries in Cleveland, TN. He has produced an extensive library of books, CDs and DVDs, and hosts *Manna-fest*, a weekly television program airing on hundreds of Christian stations nationwide. The Voice of Evangelism has a Monthly Message CD club, Partner Strike Force, and a bi-monthly magazine, which is mailed out across the nation.

Bill Cloud

Bill began studying Hebrew under the tutelage of a local rabbi and has since become quite prolific at reading and writing the Holy Tongue. He has spent many hours studying, not only the Hebrew text, but the Hebraic roots of Christianity as well. This research has been rewarded with a keen insight into Biblical Judaism and its relationship to Christianity.

Through Shoreshim Ministries, Bill and his family have launched an effort to re-introduce Christians to the Jewish Y'shua and to educate believers in the Hebraic roots of their faith. As a result of this information, disciples of the Messiah can more accurately interpret end-time events and better discern our role in these last days.

Shoreshim Ministries • 114 Stuart Rd • PMB 431 • Cleveland TN 37312
Phone: (423) 559-1177 • www.billcloud.org